Presented To:

_____

From:

_____

Date:

_____

CONQUERING *the* GAME *of* CONTROL

CONQUERING *the* GAME *of* CONTROL

Nurturing the Nature of God

DR. CRAIG A. GREEN

DESTINY IMAGE® PUBLISHERS, INC.

PO Box 310, Shippensburg, PA 17257-0310

"Promoting Inspired Lives."

This book and all other Destiny Image, Revival Press, MercyPlace, Fresh Bread, Destiny Image Fiction, and Treasure House books are available at Christian bookstores and distributors worldwide.

For a U.S. bookstore nearest you, call 1-800-722-6774.

For more information on foreign distributors, call 717-532-3040.

Reach us on the Internet: www.destinyimage.com.

ISBN TP: 978-0-7684-4095-9

ISBN Ebook: 978-0-7684-8871-5

For Worldwide Distribution, Printed in the U.S.A.

1 2 3 4 5 6 / 15 14 13 12

DEDICATION

With deepest love, I dedicate this book to my wife and ministry partner, Tina. She and I have journeyed together for over 25 years, and by God's grace a great deal of *control-ism* has died in both of us along the way. The Lord has encouraged us to delight in mutual submission and therefore the joy of genuine Christian marriage. Tina's love, support, wisdom, and sensitivity to the Holy Spirit have made this book possible. I am indebted to my wife, and all the more, to the God who allowed me to be her husband!

My deepest appreciation to...

My beautiful wife and partner in ministry, Tina, who is God's greatest gift to me. She is the reason I had the courage to write this book. Very few people have the privilege of being something of an "Aquila," married to an amazing "Priscilla." I'm one of them.

My four children—Karen, Joe, Mary Catherine, and Matthew, who are each a gift from God, and each an absolute joy to parent.

J.R. and Shirley Green—the best parents a person could ever have.

Dr. Jack Hayford, Dr. Wess Pinkham, Dr. Paul Chappell, and all the great folks at the King's Seminary for their profound teaching and loving guidance, which birthed a doctoral project and this book.

My brothers and sisters in The King's Cohort 5. I am forever grateful for the way God brought the 12 of us together. We thought it was simply about earning a D.Min., but God had, and has, so much more in mind!

Dr. Don Ragland, one of the greatest theologians I've ever met, a dear friend, and a constant source of revelational wisdom. His insights and encouragements are found throughout this book.

Dr. Robert Tuttle, an amazing scholar and theologian, and a Spirit-gifted encourager, whom God used to spur me to start—and years later—finish this project.

Rev. Rick Bonfim—an apostle, evangelist, and prophet—and a trusted friend.

Dear friends like Steve Gansel, Randy Goodman, Jon Bell, Gary Moore, and Don Morris, and to all of our treasured friends from our church families in Livingston and Lascassas.

Amy F., David, Amy O., Jennifer, Don, and Jackie—the best and most spiritually-gifted staff in any church anywhere!

Mrs. Lucile Hyder, a proofreading genius and a spiritual giant. Her amazing grasp of the English language and her love for Jesus are visible on every page.

The wonderful folks at Livingston First and Shiloh United Methodist Churches who first took part in the Rock/Paper/Scissors Curriculum. I will always appreciate your love and encouragement, and will always treasure my time as your pastor!

ENDORSEMENTS

For the past ten years, Dr. Craig Green has been my pastor and my friend. I witnessed the inception and growth of the ideas presented in these pages and have personally benefited from the teachings expounded upon in this book. I have seen the power of these truths to liberate a congregation that was deeply embroiled in control issues. This book is a valuable resource for those seeking freedom, joy, and unity in the Holy Spirit.

Dr. Don Ragland, Veterinarian
Author of *The Holy Spirit: A Layman's Perspective*

Reduce the words of Jesus to one sentence and it would have to be, "He or she who would give up their life for My sake will gain it because he or she who would be great must be servant of all, and he or she who would be first must be last." Dr. Craig Green helps us realize that this Jesus perspective is the only real antidote for the kind of control issues that lead to manipulation, intimidation, and domination. Read this book for the good of your soul and for the soul of the Church.

I've long believed that the difference between good and bad is only one or two degrees. While compassion and understanding exploit that one or two degrees in the right direction, the need for control always exploits that one or two degrees in the wrong direction. Finally, someone has exposed the subtle boundaries between compassion and control and offers us hope against despair.

Robert Tuttle
Asbury Seminary

Crises come in various shapes and sizes and never seem to let up. Drawing upon his rich experience as a pastor, Craig began to see the necessity of the dance of relationship rather than the dissonance of control. The readers of this book will recognize the fears and frustrations associated with living in a constant cycle of control/being controlled. Accordingly, *Conquering the Game of Control* is not a series of sermons or a how-to self-help book, but a set of reflections, insights, and illustrations based on a doctoral study Craig completed at The King's University. This is an insightful, authentic, and exciting book with a moving style that combines theology and practicality. It is a real book about the real world, written with warm human understanding and witty perspective. It will, and should, help many of us overcome our need to control and live from Love, not for it.

Wesley M. Pinkham
Dean of Doctoral Studies, The King's University

Amidst the intensity of life and ministry, sometimes it is difficult to remember that *"Our struggle is not against flesh and blood"* (Eph. 6:12 NASB). *Conquering the Game of Control* is a gift that enables readers to wisely discern and strategically conquer the destructive spiritual forces at work in their relationships and in their personal lives. Craig's warm candor, tempered forthrightness and deep insight will impart clarity, instill courage, and equip men and women to effectively lead with humility and authority.

Jonathan Dow, Executive Director
Aldersgate Renewal Ministries

Few authors have dared to expose the nature of deformative relationships so prevalent in the Church. Writing with the depth of a theologian and rooted in the reality of pastoral ministry, Craig Green uncovers a seductive secret rampant in the Body of Christ. This book ushers the soul into a revealing journey destined to transform both believers and congregations.

Dr. Michael R. Hawkins
Pastor, Greater Bridgeport Christian Fellowship

Craig Green is a trusted and rising voice—a true servant worthy of receiving the attention of church leaders. We all need practical and spiritually sound insight to execute our leadership tasks—sensitively and wisely, with that balance and discernment that exercises authority and boldness with a genuine humility and servant-hearted spirit. *Conquering the Game of Control* provides help—pointing the way in a manner consistent with The Way!

Jack W. Hayford
Chancellor, The King's University-Los Angeles
Founding Pastor, The Church On The Way

CONTENTS

FOREWORD

by Jack W. Hayford

A striking alteration of terms and values has occurred over the past ten years when the merit of a pastor or church officer is commendably referenced. Less than 15 years ago, an effective pastor's teaching ministry would be noted, especially if he found favor a "solid expositor." Today, he is more likely to be acknowledged for his media savvy as a "good communicator," as "being interesting" takes priority over being instructive, and the test score of one's content is less important than the ability to consistently weave interesting or humorous stories into his messages.

Similarly, a decade or two ago, the dynamic rising from a pastoral leader's focus on prayer mobilization and his passion for evangelism was worthy of elaboration, but those practices tend to be presumed and too "churchy" to mention. The consequence that flows down to a new generation is that prayer becomes a perfunctory, cosmetic exercise and passion of any depth a possible indulgence in emotionalism— unless it is targeted on a numerical increase in attendance.

The same artificial fabric mantles the mindset that becomes charmed more by a leader's church-growth strategy, highlighting its creativity in the worship and choreography and its use of media roll-ins and the way they spark interest, excitement, and expectation. Further, we can count as certain that commendation will readily be derived where the pastor has become distinguished as a source of "creative systems management" and "community-wide events garnering the goodwill of the populace"; but less likely to note or invite to speak at a conference a pastoral leader committed to cultivating a prayer-and-fasting habit as a practice, and doing so in a way that involves a significantly large part of the congregation.

By now, I fear I have reached the edge of any reader's patience—and I dearly hope I haven't lost you in what may seem a negative introduction. But, in fact, I am completely rejoiced and honored to receive Craig Green's request to provide an entrée to the valuable work you have in hand. And, whatever the risk, to begin with the observations I've made above, they are essential to help identify slippage that has become normative; accepted to the point that a slackening of basics underlies many of the methods and much of the manner of life in the 21st-century Church.

However, I am for today's Church! I love and minister to hosts of pastors and people who honestly and earnestly seek first-century dynamics to flood us at this hour when restoration is far more needed than innovation. And it is this positive belief in the timeless spiritual substance available to us all that occasions my joy over, and commendation of, this book. Something about it buttresses my confidence that we are cresting the outbreak of a wave of impending renewal of the purity and power of God's Spirit in and through the Church!

The book's theme touches the nerve of a primary and pivotal subject—spiritual authority; one of the traits that are noted at the core of Jesus' introduction of His ministry (see Matt. 7:29) and integral to His discipling of His follows as representatives of the Kingdom He was introducing (see Luke 9:1-6). It surprised people then—and it will now: the mere mention of "authority" unnerves people, but only because this fountainhead essential to all of life, being, society, maturity, and fruitfulness, is constantly embittered by human selfishness and violation of God's order in authority's exercise.

It is unsurprising that in both, the world and in the Church, there is confusion and abuse of authority. In the world it is being contested by a spirit of anarchy assailing governments everywhere—not only oppressive, abusive regimes, but challenging authority on any terms. The world is harvesting its own bitter fruit; the impact of a global society that is largely without convictions regarding absolutes or any commitment to any "truth" other than any individual's personal tastes or opinion.

My earlier observations regarding adjusted values in much of today's Church were to indicate more than "ideas"; they reflect a growing ideology. Whether codified or not, they are essentially indicative of an increasing requirement: to be "hot" in today's Church requires being "cool." At the root of style changes being made— the creeping encrustation of the casual, the culturally acceptable, preferable and comfortable, convenient and accessible approach to church life drifts away from the conclusive authority of biblical models of discipleship, worship, and Jesus' call to "take up My cross and follow Me" (see Luke 9:23).

Just as with these other terms observed—words and values being rendered passé as substitute terminology reflects an unidentified diluting of values characterizing historic evangelicalism—the word *authority* (as a reflection of a leader's style) seems to have become undesirable as well. Far better, in today's culture, to simply be a "team builder" or "highly relational" which, though worthy as a style or means of behavior, cannot alter the fact that all of life mandates that the buck stops somewhere. At the bottom line, societal resistance to authority may call for sensitivity in our description of a person who is charged with authority; but with that, there is a deep need for a recovery and a refreshed definition of spiritual leadership that is more than merely "socially preferred" or "politically correct."

Be assured, this book's message is nothing of an effort to propose either a Pharisee's brand of heavy-handed religion, but neither will you find it less than direct—forthright with needed authority and frank in denying any carnal presumption that violates the Scriptures or the Spirit of Christ among His people. Here is a sincere effort to address the deep reality of a broad and present lack of understanding the nature of spiritual authority, its source, and to address essential principles of exercise in the Church, among God's people and by spiritual leaders themselves.

Within these pages, you will find a discussion of the subject most frequently mentioned by Jesus: the Kingdom of God. It was central to His announcing the possibilities of a renewal of the divine order; God's intention for Love's dominion; the inescapable confrontation with human sin, self-will, and pride; the stark reality that spiritual warfare would be encountered—and finally, the need for structure, "under God," if you will. Thus, inescapably, the theme must flow with health, wisdom, balance, and truth into the Church's life—at least if congregations and disciples are going to band together around more than a casual commitment, a fuzzy faith, and a rendering of God's Word as a subject of transient, popular opinion rather than absolute— "The Word" that calls us to submission in all matters.

Authority and submission are inescapably pivotal concepts fundamental to biblical leadership; foundational from birth to growth, from our need to yield to God's terms of salvation to our need to grow as servants who steward the leadership of our homes, businesses, churches with an emboldened humility joined to an authority born of love—love that is rooted in the Father's heart and ministered with a firm tenderness.

Over the more than half-century I have pastored among the flock of God, I know of no theme more essential than "authority" as being critical to the understanding of church leaders or elders. Today, "leadership" is partially defined in many church settings—often only indicative of the ability to attract a crowd and keep people happy. By today's definition, "to lead" often goes only as far as leading people to salvation. However, the call to lead to the formation of disciples becomes trivialized: at its root, spiritual authority is essential to realize this task. Biblical leadership is charged with the Master's great commission; called to "teach what I have commanded you." The call is to "The Way" (it's not only to One Savior, but to a lifestyle that is absolute and "narrow").

Authority is not a shouting but a shaping—a growing of disciples under the Lordship of Christ, and unto accountable responsibility before the Word and a local assembly. It involves learning the price of bearing a mantle that doesn't tiptoe delicately around difficult or demanding issues. Neither is it demonstrated by heavy-handed or pompous preachments or tyrannical insistence on one's private opinion or pleasure. Rather, where it is discovered in the Word, developed by leaders who grow other leaders who, in partnership of life and teaching, set the table for others to witness the benevolent outcomes of God's way, will, and Word, it will effect the joyous growth of the life of Christ among a local congregation.

This is the target of this book. I heartily commend it for reading, for evaluating, and for applying to personal and congregational life. The Father's "divine order" (laws for living) is unfolded in and through the life and teaching of His Son just as certainly as the Father's "divine love" (forgiveness unto new birth) is given through His Son's death and resurrection. That love calls us to a new life—one that calls to commitment, obedience, and maturity, all three of which flow from our understanding of biblical authority.

May many be assisted from the fear that applied biblical concepts of authority will become oppressive: whatever failures of flesh or arrogance of pride have begotten such should not be allowed to sustain doubt or resistance to leading and living in the laws and ways of God. In contrast, may we all realize that: (a) soundly taught, biblical principles of authority, (b) when ministered and lived out lived by leaders who understand servant-hearted leading and mutual submission and humility among Word-centered leaders, (c) will advance today's Church to ever-increasing liberty in life, and (d) the realization of spiritual dominion and triumph through the Holy Spirit's love, truth, and life-giving presence and power. All His ways are righteousness and peace!

INTRODUCTION

Almost everyone, regardless of age or culture, knows how to play the game "Rock/Paper/Scissors." This simple game, nearly universally understood, has been played for centuries. While traveling, I often see kids—and adults—playing the game just to pass the time while waiting on a plane. With each play, someone always wins, and someone always loses. Part of the attraction is that no one wins—or loses—all the time. While paper beats rock, it can't withstand scissors; while scissors defeats paper, they can't resist the rock; while the rock dominates the scissors, it can't control the paper. Since each player has the opportunity to *control* the other—if only until the next hand—Rock/Paper/Scissors is, in the long run, an unwinnable game. Sure, there might be momentary victory, but a person cannot win at this game all the time. Still, there seems to be some sort of deep attraction to the game that keeps people playing.

I'll not take any more time describing the game; you already know all about it. But what if this simple and harmless game illustrates a not-so-harmless reality concerning the human condition? What if people are *born* a "rock"...or "paper"...or "scissors," and spend life "playing" an unwinnable game—*a game of control?* That supposition is the thesis of this book.

Some things are common to all humans—eating, drinking, breathing, and *controlling*. Ask anyone about bullies, control freaks, or power struggles, and they will have a story or ten. Controlling or being controlled is the age-long drama of every human, community, nation, tribe, and tongue. It's as if deep down inside every human is the notion that "I can be like God" (see Gen. 3:5), unconsciously motivating thoughts and actions in every area of life.

To people of faith—Jewish and Christian, there is an understanding of the source of this notion, this lie about "being God." However, little attention has been directed at how to live free from it. Thus, instead of being the place where people can find rest from bullies, control freaks, and the power hungry (and from those tendencies within themselves!), the Church is often overrun with *control-ism.*

It didn't take long in life for me to discover this reality. One of my earliest memories from school was of the bully who would walk behind me in line and kick my ankles until they were bruised. Worse yet, he went to church and Sunday school with me. I used to quietly pray that God would "get him." In a way, I guess He did. Calvin became one of my best friends in high school and college. He quit treating me like a bully and ended up being a great friend. (But not everything changed; he grew up to be a lawyer!)

Neither did it take long as a pastor to discover *controllers* in the Church. At my very first pastors' meeting, a much older and more seasoned pastor asked me about the "war department" in my church. Explaining that he meant the choir, he went on to relate horror stories about control-freak organists and choir directors. I later discovered that this pastor himself had a reputation of being a control freak. I guess it takes one to know one!

And that is one of the points of this book. We all know control-ites, bullies, and demigods, because deep down inside we *are* one, whether we want to admit it or not. It's something like a compulsion we can't fight, a game we can't help playing. But, make no mistake, this game is unwinnable; it destroys life. The purpose of this book is to expose this "game of control"; but, far more importantly, it purposes to give the way of escape. It *is* possible to quit playing this game—if we receive the right help. It *is* possible to live essentially free from the attempts of others to control us, and from our attempts to control others. The solution, however, can only be found outside of us and the deception that "you can be like God." Freedom comes when our control tendencies and our fear (or reality!) of being controlled by others is laid down before the One who has *never played control and never will*: the Lord Jesus Christ.

I invite you to join me in the discovery of the game of control and, in the process, of the grace which will lead to significant freedom from it. I assure you that I didn't write this book just to do it. This has been a burning passion in me for years. It began as God showed me my own control tendencies. It continues as I genuinely hurt for all the wounded and wounding around me—particularly in the Church—who are so close to the Answer, and yet so oblivious to the question.

Control is a horrible evil. Control is the absolute opposite of God. Control is the "elephant in the parlor" of most congregations. Control is a hopelessly addictive game we are all born to play because of our fallen nature. The only solution is to receive the power to quit playing it altogether, and that power is absolutely not human—it is divine.

Control is at the root of all genocide, rape, war, hatred, segregation, discrimination, pornography, sex trafficking, and all other forms of injustice and crime. Why? Because control is both the motivational and the operational means by which almost all sin is accomplished. Humans desire to control others, and use control upon each other. It is truly and most horrifically, a sin.

Let's begin this process together with prayer:

Father, I ask You to expose in me everything rooted in the lie that "I can be like God." I ask You to identify every technique and strategy I use to try and gain power over others. I ask You to identify everything in me which succumbs to the attempts of others to control. I ask You to forgive me and give me the grace to repent of playing this sick game. I ask You to conform me to the image of Your Son, Jesus, and His control-less life. I desire to quit playing the game! I desire to have the mind of Christ! And I acknowledge that all of my healing is found only in You, Father, Son, and Holy Spirit. Let me hear what You want me to hear and experience what You want me to experience in the reading of this book.

Finally, Father, give me the strength not to use the teaching in this book in an attempt to gain control over others. Help me not to judge others based on control types. Let me see only myself in these pages, in the Light of Your glorious restoration…in the matchless name of Jesus I pray. Amen.

Chapter One

A GAME CALLED CONTROL

I will never forget that long, miserable drive or the sick feeling I had in my gut. It was a cold, cloudy winter's day, but that wasn't the problem. *I* was the problem, and I knew it. I couldn't stand what I had just done—lied to a trusted friend, as well as the treasurer of the church I was then serving. *What kind of pastor was I? What was wrong with me? Why did this cycle keep repeating?*

Well, to the first question, I was a Spirit-filled, Jesus-loving *manipulator.* What was wrong with me was *my very nature.* And the reason this cycle of behavior kept repeating was because there was something big and deep in me that had not been surrendered to the Lordship of Jesus and the transforming power of the Holy Spirit. But I'm getting ahead of myself. Let me tell you how the truth began to dawn on me that winter's day back in 2000.

We were in the middle of something that often brings out the worst in church people, a building project. Specifically, we were remodeling our 90-year-old sanctuary. As part of that project, the board had approved the purchase of new carpet, and the treasurer was discussing that prospect with me immediately following the morning worship service. It took all of about five seconds for the discussion, from my point of view, to become uncomfortable. The treasurer was stating that a committee needed to be formed to choose the carpet style and color. Fair enough! It wasn't what he said, but how he said it, that was getting under my skin. "John" always seemed to cherish a little conflict. He enjoyed, it seemed to me, prevailing in any decision or in any relationship. Although he was and is a great guy, he liked being in charge (as if I didn't!). Life to John was like an argument, and he had to be right. Chalk it up to being tired or hurried or whatever, but I didn't want to "play." Besides, I was the *pastor.* "We'll have to do that real soon," I said to him, knowing that the carpet had already been chosen and ordered. I didn't want to fight or have to explain something at the time. Tired of being intimidated by him, I placated him temporarily...with a lie! Then, I left town for an eight-hour drive to a pastors' conference in Muncie, Indiana.

No sooner had I left than the weight of guilt and shame and self-disgust descended upon me. I spent hours in prayer and repentance. And God is good! During that time He gave me a distinct set of words, ideas, and images that form the foundation of this work. He spoke to me about my own control issues, as well as about the control-ism within all humanity. It was a powerful, life-changing experience. When I got home, I apologized to my treasurer, and then preached about the experience the next Sunday. In the years since, I have researched this topic to the point of earning my Doctor of Ministry degree writing about it. More importantly, I have experienced remarkable healing in this area, and have witnessed the same in others.

As I drove to that pastors' conference, I cried out to God about my behavior and complained about my treasurer's ability to bring out the worst in me. As I did so, God began to speak three words to me: *domination, intimidation,* and *manipulation.* Driving up I-65 that day, I realized that I was a *manipulator.* (I had manipulated the truth to my treasurer because I hated the very thing he seemed to cherish—conflict.) In turn, my treasurer was an *intimidator,* gaining control over others by frightening them—"getting in their face," so to speak. The third word, *domination,* came to mind with the remembrance of people who, like army tanks, push forward, crushing everything and everyone in their path. There, right before me, was the game we all play—Rock/Paper/Scissors!

Just as Jesus used visuals, such as a grain of wheat, to illustrate His messages, He gave me a powerful but simple picture for the relationship between domination, intimidation, and manipulation—the three sides of control. The *rock* in the game pictures domination; it dominates the *scissors*. The *scissors* correspond to intimidation, shredding the *paper* with ease but being crushed by the force of the rock. Paper represents manipulation; although it is vulnerable to scissors, it has the ability to *cover* the rock. Is this all not a parable graphically picturing the way our fallen, human control-nature works?

Because of the Fall, we are all born with, and refine through social interaction, a dominant control technique of manipulation or domination or intimidation. We play the game with each other to see who can control whom. The game, however, is unwinnable because there are always others whose control techniques "cut" us, or "crush" us, or "cover" us. In addition, there are some manipulators who are just *really* incredibly good at it. The same is true with dominators and intimidators. Furthermore, just as there are different types of control, there are different levels of ability. Moreover, we humans reserve the right to change our control style when we think it might help us prevail. The result? The absolute mess we call human nature and culture.

The world's answer is a plethora of self-help books to hone our skill and make us better at controlling. We reward with titles, finances, and accolades those who are really good at "playing the game." We celebrate those dominating personalities who bully and bruise their way to the top. We cheer on the intimidators who cut and crush and frighten and threaten—who "don't take any prisoners." We stand in awe of manipulators so masterful in their appeals that we hand over to them control (and cash!), often well before we realize (if we ever do) what has just happened to us.

We Christians, however, experience something quite different in the Church, right? Well, we should pray so; but the painful truth is that dominators, intimidators, and manipulators roam the halls of churches and Sunday schools, populate deacon boards and committee structures, and serve as pastors of almost every church. Only a few congregations—under humble leadership and greatly moved by the Holy Spirit—have collectively experienced a level of healing significantly reducing the game of control.

The regrettable truth is that most of us church people seem blissfully ignorant of how devastating the game of control is. Like the world, we actually reward the control freaks and *control-ites* in our midst. We flock to churches pastored by them, assuming that rapid growth is a sure indication of "a work of the Holy Spirit." We elect them to our boards, convinced that their abilities to control in the business world are "just what we need on the church council." Because we lack discernment about control characteristics, we confuse *charisma* with the *charismata* of the Holy Spirit.

How did we get here? Why does it seem that the Church is as ripe with control as the world around us? We need to take a deeper look biblically and see…

The Beginning of the Game

It is impossible to deny or dismiss the reality that all human life and human history are dominated by a consistent theme of conflict. One cannot listen to or read the news without being exposed to this ever-present reality. Every experience of war and aggression, every struggle between people and people groups, and every experience of discrimination, hatred, bloodshed, reprisal, marginalization, and oppression undeniably illustrates the fact that humans are in a constant state of conflict with one another. This reality is no less true in the Church. The simple truth is that congregations as ancient as the one in Corinth and as current as the most recently planted congregation experience sectarianism, division, and strife. Furthermore, what is true "within" congregations is also true "among" congregations, as evidenced by the tremendous splintering of the Body of Christ into various sects and sections throughout the Church Age.

Jews and Christians have long understood the reality of conflict as a result of the Fall of humanity. To people of faith, the brokenness of human relationships and relational ontology[1] is squarely rooted in humankind's rebellion against God and His perfect rule and reign.

As a matter of faith, believers thus recognize that the solution to the discord is beyond mere human ability to repair. To disciples of *Yeshua*, the hope of restoration is found in obedience to the Person of God in Christ Jesus, made possible by His sacrificial grace. Yet this restoration is neither instant nor absolute within the confines of the current Kingdom reality. Rebellion continues to be deeply seated within fallen humanity, but the very real and ongoing work of grace offers present help and future hope, if not an instant cure.

The fact that human conflict is rooted in original and ongoing rebellion is a matter of faith. It is the nature of the root cause of this conflict that has motivated the creation of this project. What is it that is inherent in the Fall which leads to all conflict? What fallen trait springs forth from satan's *you-can-be-like-God* lie? This author believes it is the human need to control one another—the innate desire to "be like God." Every act of violence, war, oppression, and conflict emanates from the desire to control.

Chapter three of Genesis gives people of faith a glimpse into the ontological makeup of satan, and the transfer of his nature to humanity through humanity's rebellion. Satan desired to gain control over God's highest creation—humanity and the realm of humanity's dominion, the earth. In his attempt to do so, he utilized three techniques as deeply rooted in his own being as they are totally absent from the Godhead's[2]. Satan *intimidated* Eve by appearing to her as a serpent.[3] He *manipulated* her with a deceptive question designed to create doubt about God's loving purposes.[4] Finally, in direct confrontation to God's Word, he *dominated* Eve by declaring with a usurper's authority that she would not die, but would, in fact, be like God.[5] By intimidation, manipulation, and domination, satan enticed Adam and Eve to exchange the dominion given to them as a reflection of the image their Creator God for a reflection of satan's image—control.[6]

Even as the serpent dominated, intimidated, and manipulated Eve and Adam to rebel, humans have ever since, *by nature,* done so to one another. Only the power of redemption—through the promised Seed of the woman (see Gen. 3:15)—gives us the hope that human nature can be changed. God gave the Law to His people Israel to demonstrate the fact that—without an experience literally transforming nature—all are incapable of obeying the righteousness of God because the control factor is too deeply rooted in fallen nature. Therefore, "religion," (defined as the human attempt to "get to God" as opposed to His coming to us) which always uses the (fallen) resources of domination, intimidation, and manipulation, is doomed to failure in all its forms, and is in fact satan's primary tool in keeping people trapped in the original lie.

Nowhere is the innate compulsion to control more evident than in the Gospels. It was the religious leaders' fear of losing control that drove their insane hatred for Jesus. Their use of control *intimidated* Pilate into consenting to Jesus' crucifixion while Pilate, himself, attempted to control the situation by *manipulation.*

The desire to control, variously manifested, is at the root of the endless conflict, strife, abuse, pain, affliction, and destruction—*sin*—by which humans are so often surrounded and ensnared.

The desire to be *like God*, rebellion against the one true God, is the root of our fallen human nature. Control, therefore, comes *naturally* to every human being. According to research conducted by *Leadership Magazine*, pastors in this nation report that the primary cause of conflict in the local church is the manifestation of control issues, with 85 percent of the pastors contacted reporting that control issues were the leading factors contributing to strife, conflict, and division in the local church.[7] This staggering statistic should serve as a sobering alarm to all Christians that something is seriously amiss and adrift in the life of the Church. It should break our hearts that control issues ravage and bedevil the Church at every turn and on every conceivable level.

The need for control inside and outside of church is not only a part of fallen human nature, but it is also a doorway to all kinds of demonic evil, which often flexes its muscle with special zeal in church settings. Bishop George Bloomer has identified three aspects of demonic attack that are at the heart of the warfare confronted by all believers in the spiritual realm. Equating intimidation to a terrorist tactic, manipulation with psychological warfare, and domination with the overwhelming use of power, Bloomer exposes the primary ways satan demonizes believers and demonizes others *through believers* in the thirst to control.[8]

Two major problems arise with the manifestation of control (intimidation, manipulation, and domination). First, control in and of itself is rebellion against God—witchcraft. It may come naturally to humankind, but it certainly isn't right or righteous. As Doctor Mark Rutland has emphasized, power (control) is a dangerous, demonic "game" often played with devastating effect in the American Church:

> Power games have gutted churches, destroyed ministries, and left the wives and children of pastors in quivering dysfunction. These "games" played by ruthless, remorseless rebels are nothing other or less than witchcraft in all its evil. There is a bitter irony in evangelicals up in arms over Harry Potter yet willing to tolerate without a murmur witchcraft in the choir loft.[9]

Rutland continues to address the demonic flow of control, and the way satan uses it to destroy the Church, as he shares:

> A businessman in a church I pastored used his adult Sunday school class to recruit members for a breakaway church. He twisted my words, quoted me out of context, and finally rejected the authority of the board. In a decision where the legitimate authority of the church ruled against him, he incited a knot of malcontents, excusing all his lies, false accusations, and rebellion as necessary because the pastor and board would not listen to God. Another businessman in my church said, "Well, Dr. Rutland, he is a hard-headed man." "No," I responded, "he is a witch."[10]

When one considers the perfect relationship inherent in the Godhead, and the perfected relationship offered to humans through Jesus, the cost of rebellion becomes painfully apparent. The witchcraft is the very opposite of the Spirit-indwelled and empowered relationship that is true Christianity. The lust for control becomes a channel for demonic powers to flow through persons, to the destruction of lives and even congregations, and dwarfs or destroys the relational dynamic of "being" with the Godhead. Thus, the first global problem with control-ism is that it distorts and destroys relationship with God.

A second problem associated with the manifestation of control is that controlling others is ultimately an unwinnable game, causing endless strife, pain, and division. No one *wins* all the time. *Control-ism not only distorts and destroys relationship with God, but also among human beings.* While domination may be an *effective* technique to control certain people, it has little effect on others. While an intimidator may be able to quash the desires of some people, the control technique will be ineffective and even comical to others. Like the old game of Rock/Paper/Scissors,[11] no one wins all the time.

And like that old game, one method may be highly effective in one situation but completely ineffective in another. A *Rock* may always beat *Scissors*, but it will never prevail over a *Paper*. *Paper* may always beat a *Rock*, but it will be cut to shreds by *Scissors*. Dominators are like the rock in the game. By definition, to dominate is: "To rule or control; to exert the supreme determining or guiding influence on; to occupy the most prominent position in or over something."[12] Much like a rock, dominators exert their influence and conquer by position. They are the "boulders" that push everything and everyone else out of their way. Manipulators correspond to paper. By definition, to manipulate is: "To handle or manage shrewdly and deviously for one's own profit."[13] Much as paper covers and overwhelms the rock in the game, manipulators shrewdly handle their subjects in order to control and get their way. Intimidators are like scissors. According to Webster's, to intimidate is: "To make timid or fearful; to frighten; to discourage or suppress by threats or by violence."[14] Just as scissors cut through paper with ease, intimidators cut through those they seek to control, using fear and threats to gain their advantage.

In each case, however, the control is not absolute. While a manipulator (paper) may be able to control a dominator (rock) with ease, the manipulator is in danger of being sliced to pieces by an intimidator (scissors). Each style has inherent "strengths" and "weaknesses," so that no one wins all the time. In fact, it is my desire to show that no one truly wins by playing this "game" at all. True victory only comes when the game-playing is surrendered and the motivation of the heart becomes, like Jesus, to serve in humble submission.

While relating domination, intimidation, and manipulation (control), to the game of Rock/Paper/Scissors may be unique to this author, relating these three control techniques to a *game* is not. Rod Smith, family therapist with YWAM (Youth With A Mission), has defined the same three control techniques ("cancers" of relationship) in light of a game:

> *Manipulation:* playing chess with another person or with people. Maneuvering as if life were an attempt to checkmate others into loving us or doing what we want.

> *Domination:* playing chess with another person or with people as in manipulation. The difference is the dominator has removed the opponent's pieces without declaring so in the first place.

> *Intimidation:* playing chess with another person or with people where winning and losing come with either the threat of punishment or actual punishment.[15]

Smith continues his equating of manipulation, domination, and intimidation to a twisted game by reminding his readers that in healthy relationships, "there is no element of either winning or losing; they are not a game of chess at all and are free of tactics and agenda."[16] Control is an unwinnable, ungodly game which needs to be exposed and left behind. Mutual submission as expressed in servant ministry is, in contrast, a "win-win" situation that is completely the opposite of a game; competition is replaced by mutuality and victory is defined by obedience to the Lord, not control over a fellow human.

No wonder satan approves when church people attempt to sustain their positions through the use of domination, intimidation, or manipulation. The cancerous condition emanating from fallen human nature contributes to the enemy's schemes to cripple the effectiveness of the Church by causing division, hurt, confusion, and conflict. The antithesis is the perfect relationship displayed within the Triune Godhead.

Scripture makes the antithesis clear in both general and specific ways. An antonym for domination, for example, is the biblical virtue of submission (love). While domination involves overpowering force, submission involves a willful lowering of self, a willingness to give rather than to control. Similarly, an antonym for intimidation is the biblical virtue of humility. While intimidation seeks to control through bullying and terrorizing, humility seeks to defer and avoid assertiveness or arrogance. And while manipulation involves maneuvering and conniving, an antonym would be the biblical virtue of truth, which sets people free rather than attempting to control and own them.[17]

Specifically, domination, intimidation, and manipulation correlate with the works of the flesh, outlined in Galatians 5:19-21 (see NKJV and NIV), and as opposed to the fruit of the Spirit, set forth in Galatians 5:22-23. Synonymous with domination is "contentions" and "selfish ambitions"; "discord," "dissensions," and "factions" are synonyms for manipulation; "outbursts of wrath" and "hatred" correspond to intimidation. Thus, control of others through domination, intimidation, and manipulation is a major theme in this passage, even as the antithesis to this behavior is described by the fruit of the Spirit.[18]

Thus, to have the mind of Christ as outlined in Philippians 2 involves humility, mutuality, obedience, and esteem for others, as opposed to the pursuit of one's own goals through control. The relationship within the Godhead is utterly devoid of any work of the flesh, any selfishness, and anything resembling control.

How does a local church specifically, and the universal Church generally, move believers away from games of control in interpersonal relationships to a place of mutual submission expressed in servant ministry? How does any local church help people to repent from the practices of domination, manipulation, or intimidation and instead relate to one another in love, with the mind of Christ? These are the questions that drove me to write this book, and I hope they are the questions that you, my readers, will ponder.

The Church of Jesus Christ is worldwide experiencing unparalleled growth and an amazing season of supernatural signs and wonders. Yet, at the same time, millions of believers have been wounded. Church members have been wounded by their leaders; leaders by church members; and church members by one another. It's no wonder that millions have opted to get out altogether. Overwhelmingly, these ex-church members (and pastors) will continue to express a love for Jesus, but not for His Church. And amazingly, both the hurting and the hurt-causing continue to operate in controlling ways guaranteed to continue the cycle.[19]

It is high time for the game to end! It is time we call control what it is—*sin*! The Church, individually and collectively, needs to repent of Nicolaitans (dominators), Balaamites (manipulators), and Jezebels (intimidators). "Ephesians Christianity" can once again be the standard in the Church only when the Church—leaders and laity— recognize control for what it is, address it in terms of repentance, and then walk in the freedom that comes from deliverance.

Seven Churches, Three Control Types

All three major control issues are cited by Jesus in the letters to the seven churches of Asia. First, domination is seen in the *"deeds of the Nicolaitans"* (Rev. 2:6). The word *Nicolaitans* actually means "to conquer the laity," thus speaking of a dominating of the *laos.* Second, manipulation is clearly manifest in the *"doctrine of Balaam"* (Rev. 2:14). Unable to curse Israel directly, Balaam had to resort to manipulation, seducing the Israelites into sexual immorality (see Num. 22:1–25:3). Third, intimidation is seen in Jezebel, who clearly operated in this control-style (see Rev. 2:20). In order to get her way, she intimidated everyone around her, especially Ahab and even Elijah (see 1 Kings 16; 19; 2 Kings 9). Reminding the churches of the importance of hearing "what the Spirit says to the churches," Jesus called the seven churches to a place of recognition, repentance, and regeneration—particularly in terms of domination, intimidation, and manipulation. Oh that the Church today would hear what the Spirit is saying in regard to all three forms of control-ism! I believe that the Lord's call to recognition, repentance, and regeneration concerning control-ism continues to all the Church in this present hour.

Although there seems to be at least some understanding within the Church concerning the problem of control-ism, there appears to be little specific teaching or programming designed to actually help people recognize and repent so that regeneration can take place. As Henri Nouwen once observed, "It seems easier to be God than to love God, easier to control people than to love people."[20]

This book has been undertaken because of the obvious lack of how-to information for being set free from control-ism. Its purpose is to give a teaching that can be implemented to help people to be set free from control-ism. Chapters Six through Twelve are actually the outlines of a teaching series I developed to raise awareness of and to focus the Church on this overwhelming problem, as well as to help believers lay down their control-ism and instead "submit to one another in the fear of God" (see Eph. 5:21). Not surprisingly, I titled the series "The Rock/Paper/Scissors Curriculum." It was developed and tested, with gratifying results, in a church setting. Hopefully, the book will be helpful to other pastors and their members. The goal is transformed lives—lives less controlling and controlled, lives more submitted and servant-like.

Earlier, we indicated some ignorance about the facets of control-ism. It seems that our culture may be more aware of the problem of control-ism than today's Church. Of course, I do not think the Church should follow the culture. The Church should be the instrument of God to transform the culture. However, it should concern us that the academic disciplines of leadership development, human relations, and psychology seem to take control issues more seriously than the Church does. For example, a recent article in *U.S. News and World Report* entitled "Bad News for Bullies" addressed the issue with surprising clarity. In the article, David Gergen, noted the following:

> Surveys also find that of all the complaints people have about their work, from low pay to long hours, the biggest single one is that of the bully boss...Yet there is a distinctly different form of leadership that has arisen in recent years, represented by Bill Thomas, the cofounder of Eden Alternative...Thomas is a living symbol of what is called the

"servant leader." In the burgeoning literature about how best to lead, Robert K. Greenleaf famously coined that phrase in an essay titled "The Servant as Leader." In the years since, Greenleaf's ideas have drawn a sizable following, and their echoes have appeared in popular leadership books by Stephen Covey, Ken Blanchard, Max Dupree, and others.[21]

While we should argue that it was Jesus, not Greenleaf, who coined the concept, if not the phrase, "the servant as leader," we cannot deny that the secular world has a significant understanding of a problem that plagues all humanity, and embarrassingly so, the Church.

Servant-leadership, it appears, plays a significant role in advancing people and companies from a place of competence to a place of excellence. In his best-selling book *Good to Great*, Jim Collins discusses what he terms "Level 5 Leadership." He points out the following:

> We were surprised, shocked really, to discover the type of leadership required for turning a good company into a great one. Compared to high-profile leaders with big personalities who make headlines and become celebrities, the good-to-great leaders seem to have come from Mars. Self-effacing, quiet, reserved, even shy—these leaders are a paradoxical blend of personal humility and professional will. They are more like Lincoln and Socrates than Patton or Caesar.[22]

If the culture around us can identify servant-leadership and the problems of control, surely the Church can as well and additionally provide the real answers as to how one can become a great leader—*a servant-leader*—significantly freed from the desire to control as well as the propensity of being controlled by others. This book is dedicated to that end.

Psychologists and sociologists have researched the concept of a "locus (location) of control" for over 50 years. According to the research, people have either an *internal* locus of control and thus perceive that their actions and behavior give them the ability to control situations and people, or have an *external* locus of control and have little faith in their own ability to control situations, believing that fate or God or something else is in control. In this framework, control is a given; the only question is whether a person locates that control within or without themselves. Again, this book is dedicated to a third option: that control—within and without—can be replaced by a deep sense of trust in a God who never *controls* anyone![23]

Back to that long drive to Indiana… Not only did the Lord show me the correlation between the game of Rock/Paper/Scissors and the human control traits of domination/manipulation/intimidation, but He also gave me a Scripture reference—chapters four and five of Ephesians. If believers were truly equipped—matured and mended, they would grow up, be less likely to toss others "to and fro," and be less likely themselves to be tossed to and fro!

Although maturity in the Lord is necessary for repenting of and growing away from our basic control nature, what we are growing *toward* is far more important than what we are growing away from. *"Submitting one to another, in the fear of God"* (Eph. 5:21) describes what mature Christian relationships should look like—submission is service-based, not control-based. With this framework in place, I began a journey of scriptural research which, over the next eight years, led to the writing of this book. While I hope you at least ponder what I received as a "download" that day in my car, I want to assure you that what I'm sharing with you is biblical truth in which you can place real trust. If it weren't, it would be of no value. Scripture, however, gives us a tremendous look into the character and nature (ontology) of both God and one of His creatures—lucifer. As we contrast the two, we'll see better the source of control and the reality that God has nothing to do with it!

A Stern Warning

Being human, control comes quite naturally to all of us. That includes a huge urge, when confronted with the teaching in this book, to label and judge others based on their control-nature preferences. This is particularly true of those we are closest to (like our spouses) as well as those who irritate us the most in their use of control, like co-workers, bosses, and so forth.

Let me offer an admonition for reading the rest of this work: *Please* fight the urge to think about anyone other than yourself in terms of control! You cannot change anyone else: You are responsible only for confronting your own fallen nature and turning to the One who can transform it. Using the premise of this book as a weapon against another person is just a sorry exercise in control! Please refrain from it. Instead, may I suggest serious introspection while reading this book—introspection which leads to repentance and transformation within and to compassion and tolerance toward others! Let the Lord Jesus deal with their issues; after all, He alone is Lord, and we are definitely not!

Chapter Two

A MATTER OF CHARACTER

I have the privilege of being "Fred's" pastor. Fred, in his mid-fifties, is a remarkable person to anyone who has eyes to see his heart. Several in this little town, however, judge him by outward appearance and his past. Since Fred was conceived in incest, his mother—understandably—abandoned him to be raised by his grandparents. Lacking proper parental guidance along with being mentally challenged, he became the town drunk and town flasher. His language could vie with that of any sailor, and he spent many a night in the local jail. He was also a frequent visitor, usually unwelcome, in most of the churches in town. He finally came to the church I serve, where he wasn't asked to leave. He was welcomed and—when ready—prayed for. In a dramatic experience of healing at the altar of the sanctuary one night, several vile and demonic things left Fred; and the presence of the Lord filled those voids.

I became Fred's pastor a few years after his Holy-Spirit deliverance. I'll never forget the night I was given the eyes to see Fred for who he really is. The small congregation in a Sunday-night service had gathered in a circle to pray at the close of the service. Head bowed and eyes closed, I was startled to hear a baritone voice praying with unusual depth and authority. I couldn't help peeking to see who was praying so beautifully. Although not gifted at speech, Fred was praying with great fervor, obviously in God's favor! Though his sins had been as scarlet, they were white as snow; though they had been red like crimson, they were as wool (see Isa. 1:18). Once the town drunk and town flasher, he was now a mighty man of prayer. Only God can do that!

One of the most obvious and most amazing evidences that people have truly come into relationship with Jesus is the reality that their very character changes. Truly, we *"know them by their fruits"* (Matt. 7:16). No longer driven by the *"works of the flesh,"* they begin to exhibit *"fruit of the Spirit"* (Gal. 5:19,22), the *fruit* becoming ever and ever more obvious in their lives. Even as we shrink in horror when confronted by those bound up in demonic character, we laud and honor those who have developed a godly character, not by effort but by *"beholding…the glory of the Lord"* (2 Cor. 3:18). Even as I am repelled and chagrined when I look back 25 years in my own life, I am amazed at the change that has been wrought in me.

Before Jesus, I was a drinking, drugging, lust-driven, selfish, narcissistic jerk. By the way, I was also a faithful member of the church. What happened to me, in a story that could be another book, was an experience of *revelation* that forever changed me. I suddenly knew—I mean *knew*—that Jesus is God, Jesus is alive, and Jesus loves me. That revelation changed everything! As with all true revelation, it was a supernatural grace-gift from Father, Son, and Holy Spirit. *Churchianity* gave way to Christianity, *religiosity* to relationship. Sometimes with breathtaking speed, but mostly by imperceptible shifts, my character has changed "from glory to glory." The more I walk with God, the more I seem to talk like, think like, act like, love like, and even *smell* like Him! (See Second Corinthians 2:15.) The more I walk in submission to God, the less I'm prone to control like satan.

Control-ism is a profound character flaw. That control-ism can be removed and replaced by submission and servant ministry by the grace (supernatural power) of Christ is foundational to a sound understanding of the meaning of the Gospel of Jesus Christ.

However, to really understand the gain found in the exchange the Gospel offers, we need to understand the loss perpetuated by the

Fall. As Dr. Robert Tuttle has said, "Too many of us simply don't know what we're missing, because we do not realize what we had."[1] In the beginning, humankind was created in the image of God—an image John Wesley termed "original righteousness."[2] Adam and Eve were originally righteousness-prone rather than sin-prone! Since their fall, however, everyone has been born sin-prone. The good news of Jesus Christ is that, by grace and through faith, we can experience the supernatural power of God in Christ Jesus to move "from glory to glory" toward what was lost in the Fall. We can become more prone to obey than to sin, more inclined to love than to hate, and more eager to seek righteousness than rebellion. God gives the *power to become* His sons to all who are born *"nor of the will of the flesh, nor of the will of man, but of God"* (John 1:13).

The reality of human character becoming like the Lord's is built upon the fact that *God has a character.* He has a nature, a *being*—a way of living, relating, and thinking. The wonderful truth is that He has a magnificent, astonishing, perfect character! His *ontology* has been revealed to us, and is, of course, *the* model of perfect love, relationship, unity, submission—of Life!

On the other hand, satan also has a character, and his ontology has also been revealed. Even as each aspect of the "fruit of the Spirit" manifests of the character of Christ, the "works of the flesh" manifest the character of satan. His character is the total and absolute opposite of God's character. Everything the Father, Son, and Holy Spirit is, satan is not! Satan is the diametric opposite of God. In his attempt to confuse his nature with God's nature, he presents, in grotesque distortion, a pathetic faux-trinity of beast, antichrist, and false prophet. In contrast to God's glorious authority, sovereignty, and power, satan rules awkwardly and rudely through domination, manipulation, and intimidation.

The problem is that, until salvation and sanctification have begun a significant transformation in us, we are, *by nature and character,* more like satan than like God. As we look at the stark difference between the perfect and the fallen character, we'll begin to recognize the beauty and glory of God's ontology, as well as the ugly, controlling counterfeit of satan's.

Defining "Ontology"

I have used (and will use again) the term *ontology*. Simply, the word means to study "the being," the nature and character, of a person.[3] God has a nature worthy of study. His very being, His very nature and character, His personality, and His temperament have all been revealed to us in the Word, both in the printed Word and in the Incarnate Word, Jesus. Satan also has a character and nature, also revealed in Scripture.

Although the first Adam was created with God's nature, he took on satan's nature when he sinned. He traded a perfect nature and relationship for the lies of control—lies that he could be like God, that he could reign in his own life, and that he could reign over others. Furthermore, he has passed his fallen nature down to all humankind. Adam trashed his original ontological reality which in turn mangled ours!

The good news is that the Second Adam, who created the first Adam, *is* God; and, by resisting every temptation of satan, retained His ontological perfection all the way through the cross. The promise is that every disciple and all of creation will one day be restored to God's perfection. His ontology will define all! This is the essence of the Gospel, and it is succinctly expressed in the first textbook printed in America:

> In Adam's fall, we sinned all.
> Heaven to find / The Bible mind.
> Christ crucify'd / For sinners dy'd.[4]

Boyhood Ontological Challenges

I grew up on a typical block in Hays, Kansas. On our block there were about 20 houses and about that many kids. There was one kid in particular who made it his goal to get the rest of us in trouble. He was a leader, a bully, and the type of guy you didn't want to cross. He was famous (infamous!) with the neighborhood kids because, among other things, he almost burned down his own house (playing with matches) at the age of four. He introduced us to "girly" magazines, dirty language, and petty crime. He led us into many questionable, dangerous, and even unlawful activities—all before any of us were in our teens! His ontological makeup had a definite impact on those of us who grew up around him! Like metal to a magnet, his ontological makeup was also strangely attractive to us.

Fortunately, my parents, and most of the others in our neighborhood, were "on" to him. They kept a close eye on us if we spent too much time with "Diablo." Furthermore, a saintly lady on the block also kept an eye on all the kids in the neighborhood. Bold enough to steer us in the right direction when we were out of line, she corrected, comforted, and confronted those of us fortunate enough to grow up around her. Although I admired and loved Mrs. Westphal, I couldn't help being drawn to the ways of *diablo*.

What was true on my home block in Hays, no doubt, is a typical picture of life. Infinitely magnified, it depicts the difference between satan's warped ontology and God's perfect being. It also portrays our *natural* inclinations. We may admire God, but we lust for the things of satan, unless and until we are born again into a place where God's ontology attracts us and we begin to change. The Holy Spirit (like Mrs. Westphal) confronts and convicts us to lead us toward new birth and through to new life in Christ Jesus. Without the Spirit's powerful wooing, filling, and healing, we would be held forever as hostages to our natural lusts. Even with His help, we by nature falter...*a lot.*

The Character of God

Before we begin to look at the character of God, I want to make it clear that I believe Scripture is the only place where we start with an absolute sense of stability, authenticity, and reliability. I have been a Scripture-rooted believer ever since I first recognized Jesus for who He is. When Jesus became *Jesus* to me, *Scripture* became *Jesus*! I know the reaction to this statement might be "No, preacher, the Scripture is and has always been, *the Scripture.*" Yes, but until we have revelation knowledge, we'll never be able to move from knowing to *Knowing,* from hearing to *Hearing,* from belief to *Faith.*

Remember what Jesus said to Peter after his declaration that Jesus was *"the Christ, the Son of the living God"* (Matt. 16:16)? He wasted no time in sharing that Peter's conviction had not been revealed "by flesh and blood, but by my Father, who is in Heaven" (see Matt. 16:17). God the Father Himself had made Jesus' identity known to Peter! That's revelation knowledge, not just intellectual assent! That's the real joy of Christianity, isn't it? It's not some dry theology or boring religion. Once and for all, Christianity is not a religion at all; it's a relationship with Father, Son, and Holy Spirit. Because Jesus is real, alive, and fully God, we get to…

> really personally,
> truly experientially,
> absolutely scripturally,
> deeply and intimately,
> incredibly intellectually,
> powerfully traditionally,
> completely contemporarily,
> KNOW GOD!

This always-changing but never-changing *relationship* with God called *Christianity,* is more exciting and more rewarding than anything the world has to offer. I just needed to get that off my chest. Now that I've made clear my unwavering belief that Scripture is Jesus, let's begin our examination of what *Jesus* says about His very nature and character.

All Trinity, No Control

Let's begin with the obvious: God is Father, Son, and Holy Spirit; He is Three with distinctness and definition, yet One indivisible being. We all recognize that the revelation of God's Triune nature *(and it is scriptural revelation, not just a theological creation!)* is impossible for us finite humans to fully grasp. Nevertheless, it is critical that we begin to get a grip on the concept. Without recognizing and relating to the Threeness-in-Oneness of God, it is impossible to understand His character and nature.

All cults, heresies, and false religious systems deny or attack the Triune nature of Father, Son and Holy Spirit. Hating the relationship God has within Himself, satan fights visciously to deny it. The devil can't stand real relationship—and Father, Son, and Holy Spirit are in *perfect* relationship. Therefore, satan pushes religious substitutes that are always built upon the denial of the foundational truth of the relationship within God Himself!

Both the Old and New Testaments have a number of references to the Triune God. Standing alone, however, none of them fully develops the Trinitarian theology that helps differentiate true Christianity from various heresies, sects, and religions. Taken together, these Scriptures present a powerful revelation of the Triune Godhead. For example, Jacob prayed a beautiful Trinitarian prayer over Joseph in Genesis 48:15-16, invoking the blessing of the God of Abraham and Isaac, of God, his Shepherd, and of God, the Angel. Father, Son, and Holy Spirit, by any other name, still smell as sweet! In another example, the birth narratives of Jesus reveal the active presence of all three members of the Godhead. The same is true of Jesus' baptism: God the Son rose up out of the water, God the Holy Spirit descended upon Him as a dove, and God the Father spoke His affirmation from Heaven (see Matt. 3:16-17). Later, as Jesus was preparing to return to the Father, He admonished the disciples to make disciples of all nations, *"baptizing them in the name of the Father and of the Son and of the Holy Spirit"* (Matt. 28:19).

In reference to this passage, Dallas Willard challenges believers not to reduce the great commission to a baptismal formula. In his paraphrase, which highlights the Trinitarian revelation contained in the passage, he writes:

> I have been given say over all things in heaven and in the earth. As you go, therefore, make disciples of all kinds of people, submerge them in Trinitarian Presence, and show them how to do everything I have commanded. And now look: I am with you every minute until the job is done.[5]

As Willard rightly expresses, the common error is to focus on baptism as a ritual, or on "in the name of the Father, Son, and Holy

Spirit" as a formula, missing the point that believers can and must be "wet"—and stay wet—with the Triune presence of God.

The New Testament gives other instances where Jesus spoke of the Father and the Spirit within the same thought or context.[6] For example, John records that He spoke of the Spirit of Truth proceeding from the Father (see John 15:26). And, in His Word through Paul, we have one of the clearest and most concise Trinitarian Scriptures: *"The grace of the Lord Jesus Christ, and the love of God, and the communion of the Holy Spirit be with you all. Amen"* (2 Cor. 13:14). Taken together, the scriptural references and inferences to the Trinity are clear and compelling.

It should also be noted that the Trinitarian reality is introduced early in the Bible—actually in the first three verses. In *Christianity 101*, Gilbert Bilezikian says, "We do not have to go very far into the Bible to discover that God is a trinity of persons within one being."[7]

He continues:

In Genesis 1:1, we are introduced to God as the one who conceives and designs the works of creation. Because He is the mastermind behind creation and the One who generates the universe, we recognize Him as the Father of lights from whom derives every good and perfect gift (cf. James 1:17). In the first sentence of the Bible, God is presented as the Father and originator of the created world.[8]

Moving to the next verse, Bilezikian shares:

In Genesis 1:2, we are introduced to God as the Spirit who watches over the works of creation in His role of protector and perfecter. In this verse, God is identified as the Spirit of God.[9]

Finally, Bilezikian adds:

In Genesis 1:3, we are introduced to the "Word" of God through whose agency God's will becomes activated. God speaks, and the Word makes it happen. This is the Word who was in the beginning, who was with God who was God, and who was one with the Father. Through Him all things were made and, eventually, He became flesh and lived among us as the Son who had come from the Father (cf. John 1:1-18). In Genesis 1:3, we are introduced to God the Son.[10]

The Trinitarian nature of God shows up again in the first chapter of Genesis. In verse 26, we read: *"God said, 'Let Us make man in Our image, according to Our likeness....'"* As stated earlier, it takes further revelation and a living relationship with the "Us" and the "Our" of the passage to more fully recognize this reality. Eastern Orthodox Christianity, with its strong emphasis on the early Church councils, is particularly firm in advocating the Triune essence of this passage. As Timothy Ware states:

God speaks in the plural: "Let Us make man." The creation of the human person, so the Greek Fathers continually emphasized, was an act of all three persons in the Trinity, and therefore the image and likeness of God must always be thought of as a *Trinitarian* image and likeness.[11]

Thus, even from the first words of Scripture, we see the Triune nature and character of God and the clear ontological transfer of that nature and character in the creation of humanity.

As well as keeping in mind the three Persons of the Trinity, we should also understand the concept that the Godhead has no beginning or end. Note what Thomas Oden has shared:

How can the Son be begotten before time? There is no before with Him. The Logos that is eternal by definition must exist before time. This is hardly an optional point of Christian theology. Far from being a tardy accretion of hellenization, the seeds of this premise were firmly embedded in the earliest Christian preaching, for how could the Son be born in time or sent from the Father on a mission to the world if the Son had no life with the Father before nativity?[12]

The Father and Son have always been, as has the Holy Spirit. They are coeternal, and preexistent. Pre- what? *Pre-everything!* Oden continues, "Ancient ecumenical teaching holds that the Son is the second of three coequal, distinguishable, but inseparable persons of the triune Godhead, coeternal with the Father and the Spirit."[13]

Make no mistake. We serve a Triune God, Three, yet One; One, yet Three, with love and life so perfectly awesome and full as to be completely sufficient within Himself.

God Loves to Dance!

My father, J.R. Green, loved ballroom dancing. He was quite good at it, and I still marvel at the coordination and choreography necessary for two people to dance together in an apparently effortless and beautiful fashion. Dad would hum a tune and dance with one of us kids—there are six of us—or with Mom (also a good dancer) across the living room floor. Those will always be precious memories to me, although I don't claim to have inherited Dad's gift of dancing!

Millions enjoy watching others dance (or attempt to dance!) on television, and millions enjoy dancing themselves. There is a beauty almost indescribable when two people become one on the dance floor. It is a truly spiritual experience. And rightly so—God, Himself, danced! In fact, He is waltzing as One this very moment!

The early Church fathers, particularly the Cappadocian Fathers, understood that God is a perfect dancer. Perfectly, eternally, and effortlessly, God dances—not a solo, not a twosome, but a *Threesome*, yet so fully intertwined as to be inseparably One. The early Church fathers called this divine dance *perichoresis* (divine choreography). Father, Son, and Holy Spirit enjoy the perfect choreography of perfect relationship moving in flawless rhythm, faultless timing, absolute coordination, always perfectly in tune with each other—Three yet perfectly One.[14]

Try to get hold of this word picture, one the early Church understood so well. *Our God dances!* He does so in such perfection that He is truly, eternally One. It was, and is, and will always be His greatest desire to dance the dance of perfect relationship with us humans—His highest and most treasured creation! No wonder

Zephaniah 3:17 describes the Lord our God dancing over us, His people, His beloved "Daughter of Zion"!

Adam and Eve witnessed the *perichoresis*—this divinely choreographed dance, this twirl and dip and bow of perfect relationship—*in* God. Their lives, prior to the Fall, were a continuous perichoresis *with* God and each other. They lost it, however, when they ate of the forbidden fruit, the dance replaced by the antithesis of *perichoresis*: selfish, unchoreographed, uncoordinated control. Consequently, the perichoresis was lost to all humanity until Jesus *danced* His way into humanity. Now, once again, humans can dance with God, if they are willing to let Him do the leading.

It should not surprise us that satan does not want us to *dance* with God, or with each other. In fact, he doesn't even want us to know the dance is possible. That's why he has relentlessly attacked the very nature of God in every heresy and cult down through the ages. Satan loves it when we *religiously* believe a lie about God and ourselves. Because he hates "the dance" within the Godhead, he constantly slanders His very nature. Because he hates the possibility of humans dancing with God, he relentlessly lies about the very possibility. Satan hopes, of course, that we will, in line with our fallen nature, behave like him, thereby failing to discover the dance of God's nature, or the nature of God's dance. Because he so desperately wants to be God, he has come up with an unholy trinity of domination, intimidation, and manipulation: the *beast*, the *false prophet*, and the *dragon* of Revelation 16:13! However, we've read the end of the story: we know that satan will never measure up against God's perfect sovereignty.

Heresies and the Cappadocian Fathers

Heresies always begin with a diminishing of the Trinity. Each of them, old and new, is simply another manifestation of the ontology of satan, another manifestation of his unholy trinity of domination, manipulation, and intimidation. Every argument that attempts to diminish the perfect relationship within the Godhead is a manifestation of control, satan lying about and against the Almighty God.[15] Thomas

Oden has compiled a list of some of the early heresies. Note that in every case, the character and nature of Jesus, and therefore the Godhead, was under attack:

Heresies that rejected Christ's humanity:

Docetists (Christ as not fully in flesh)

Apollinarians (*Logos* replaces human spirit)

Eutychians (Christ as a single, mixed nature)

Heresies that reject Christ's divinity:

Eutychians (Christ not fully divine, but mixed nature)

Ebionites (Jesus as natural son of Joseph and Mary)

Arians (Christ as creature, not eternal)

Heresies that reject Christ's personal union:

Nestorians (Christ as two persons)[16]

A striking example of God "working all things together for good" is the fact that heresies in the early years of the Christian faith led to the most powerful and descriptive revelations concerning the nature of God. These Trinitarian revelations, expressed in shorthand in the Nicene Creed, are startlingly fresh in our day. In the same way that we can be thankful for the times of persecution that bring us to greater maturity, clarity, and reliance upon God, we can be thankful for those brilliant and insightful declarations of the Cappadocian Fathers.

The Cappadocian Fathers, so named because they were from the province of Cappadocia in Asia, are recognized as defenders, clarifiers, and definers of the Christian faith, especially regarding the ontology of the Holy Trinity. These three leaders were Basil the Great, Gregory of Nazianzus, and Gregory of Nyssa.[17] These three have been credited above all others in the defeat of the Arian heresy at the Constantinople Council, A.D. 381.[18] Joining the Cappadocians in this effort was Athanasius of Alexandria, who had defended Trinitarian truth at the first Nicene Council (325). Timothy Ware wrote the following of them:

It was the supreme achievement of St. Athanasius of Alexandria to draw out the full implications of the key word in the Nicene Creed: *homoousios,* one in essence or substance, consubstantial. Complementary to his work was that of the three Cappadocian Fathers, Saints Gregory of Nazianzus, known in the Orthodox Church as Gregory the Theologian (?329-?90), Basil the Great (?330-79), and his younger brother Gregory of Nyssa (died 394). While Athanasius emphasized the unity of God—Father and Son are one essence *(ousia)*—the Cappadocians stressed God's threeness: Father, Son, and Holy Spirit are three persons *(hypostasis)*. Preserving a delicate balance between the threeness and the oneness in God, they gave full meaning to the classic summary of Trinitarian doctrine, *three persons in one essence*. Never before or since has the Church possessed four theologians of such stature within a single generation.[19]

Ware is also helpful in relating the essence of the Arian heresy which prompted these four gifted saints to write in revelational understanding concerning the nature of God:

> The main work of the Council of Nicaea in 325 was the condemnation of Arianism. Arius, a priest in Alexandria, maintained that the Son was inferior to the Father, and, in drawing a dividing line between God and creation, he placed the Son among created things: a superior creature, it is true, but a creature none the less. His motive, no doubt, was to protect the uniqueness and the transcendence of God, but the effect of his teaching, in making Christ less than God, was to render impossible our human deification. Only if Christ is truly God, the council answered, can He unite us to God, for none but God Himself can open to humans the way of union. Christ is 'one in essence, *(homoousios)* with the Father. He is no demigod or superior creature, but God in the same sense that the Father is God: 'true God from true God,' the council proclaimed in the Creed which it drew up, 'begotten not made, *one in essence* with the Father'.[20]

That the Cappadocian Fathers had a dramatic and lasting impact on the direction of the Christian faith is undeniable.[21] That God the

Father, Son, and Holy Spirit used them to clarify and give language and definition to what the Scriptures had already revealed is a matter of broad-based faith and belief. What may be less known is the impact of Saint Basil's sister Macrina. Dale Irvin and Scott Sunquist have written:

> The fourth member of this theological circle was Basil's elder sister Macrina (327-380). When she was only twelve, the man to whom she had been promised in marriage died. Freed from the engagement made in her name, Macrina opted for a life of celibacy that allowed her to devote both time and money to furthering the cause of the gospel. With her mother, she founded a monastic community for women in their home. Gregory describes his older sister several times as being his teacher, and Gregory of Nazianzus indicates as much as well. Although she did not write any works of her own, apparently her influence within the circle touched upon issues of both spirituality and doctrine.[22]

It seems especially important to me that God would choose to use both males and females at this critical juncture in the life of His Body, the Church, since *"male and female He created them"* (Gen. 1:27b). The heart and crux of the argument the Cappadocian Fathers (and Mothers!) were dealing with was the very being of God Himself, and its importance in enabling humanity's restoration to original righteousness.

In the words of the Cappadocian Fathers, we find some of the most revealing and revered words ever written concerning the true identity of the Holy Trinity. As to the ontology of God, the Cappadocians remind us:

> (We proclaim) precisely and simply the doctrine of God the Trinity, comprehending out of Light (the Father), Light (The Son), in Light (The Holy Ghost)...Was and Was and Was, but Was One Thing, Light thrice repeated, but One Light...In Thy Light shall we see Light.[23]

This revelational truth is repeated by multiple millions of believers weekly in the pronouncing of the Nicene Creed, as the faithful proclaim belief "in one Lord, Jesus Christ, the only Son of God, eternally begotten of the Father, God from God, *Light from Light*, true God from true God…"[24]

Again, Gregory the Nazianzen reminds us that,

> The Trinity is a true Trinity; not a numbering of unlike things, but a binding together of equals. Each of the Persons is God in the fullest sense. The Son and the Holy Ghost have their source of Being in the Father, but in such sense that They are fully consubstantial with Him, and that neither of Them differs from Him in any particular Essence.[25]

That the Father, Son, and Holy Spirit are "consubstantial" reveals the deeply interconnected and interpenetrating reality of pure relationship—that they are truly and perfectly of one nature and kind.

Saint Basil gets to the heart of what consubstantial *(homoousios)* means as he spoke concerning the very being of the Holy Spirit— "unapproachable in thought," exactly as are the Father and Son. Basil said:

> Moreover the surpassing excellence of the nature of the Spirit is to be learned not only from His having the same title as the Father and the Son, and sharing in their operations, but also from His being, like the Father and the Son, unapproachable in thought. For what our Lord says of the Father as being above and beyond human conception, and what He says of the Son, this same language He uses also of the Holy Ghost.[26]

Being "above and beyond" human conception, the Godhead's ontological makeup defies human verbiage. However, the Cappadocian Fathers' attempts to define the concept in a way that could be humanly conceived are without parallel. As Gregory of Nyssa, in writing for all three (and for all Trinitarians) shared:

> What, then, is our doctrine? The Lord, in delivering the saving Faith to those who became disciples of the word, joins with the Father and the Son and the Holy Spirit also; and we affirm that the union of that which has once been joined

is continual; for it is not joined in one thing, and separated in others. But the power of the Spirit, being included with the Father and the Son in the life-giving power, by which our nature is transferred from the corruptible life to immortality, and in many other cases also, as in the conception of "Good," and "Holy," and "Eternal," "Wise," "Righteous," "Chief," "Mighty," and in fact everywhere, has an inseparable association with them in all the attributes ascribed in a sense of special excellence. And so we consider that it is right to think that that which is joined to the Father and the Son in such sublime and exalted conceptions is not separated from them in any. For we do not know of any differences by way of superiority and inferiority in attributes which express our conceptions of the Divine nature, so that we should suppose in an act of piety (while allowing to the Spirit community in the inferior attributes) to judge Him unworthy of those more exalted. For all the Divine attributes, whether named or conceived, are of like rank one with another, in that they are not distinguishable in respect of the significance of their subject.[27]

This declaration of the unity and equality within the Godhead is foundational to true Trinitarian revelation. Without equality within the Godhead, there can be no Divine Dance, no godly choreography, no *perichoresis*. As Gregory of Nyssa so articulately shares, however, there *is* equality within divinity. Father, Son, and Holy Spirit cannot be separated in terms of glory or in terms of chronology. Almighty God, in all of His self-being, is "Good" and "Holy" and "Eternal" and "Wise." He cannot be separated from Himself. He cannot be divided. He cannot be except what He "be."

This truth that God the Father, Son, and Holy Spirit are consubstantial, three *personas*, yet One God, is foundational to any discussion concerning the very nature of God. The beauty and intricacy of the *perichoretic* (divine-dancing) relationship within God, as seen in the prior quotes, was magnificently realized and expressed by the Cappadocians. Yet, as with all truth, what the Cappadocians expressed, God through Scriptures had already revealed. Believers of every age have known by *relational revelation*[28] the same truth, although most have lacked the verbiage and insight to express that reality as well as did the Cappadocian Fathers.

Many have written powerfully and decisively concerning the ontology of the Godhead, both before and after Athanasius of Alexandria, Gregory of Nazianzus, Basil the Great, and Gregory of Nyssa. For example, both Polycarp and Ignatius of Antioch wrote in explicitly Trinitarian ways in the early 100s.[29] Both Athenagoras and Theophilus wrote in defense and in explanation of the Triune reality before 180.[30] Likewise, Tertullian and Origen wrote detailed and eloquent treatises concerning the Trinity around 215.[31] What is obvious in their writings is not only their own relational revelation concerning the scriptural presentation of the Trinity, but also the fact that they were stating arguments that were already widely circulating.[32]

Clearly, the true ontology of God did not just spring forth in the fourth century: it was taught by Jesus, confirmed by the Spirit, revealed in Scripture, and relationally understood by multitudes long before the Nicene Creed was written. Disciples of every generation, engaged in the relational dance with God, have struggled to find fresh verbiage to describe the eternal ontology of Eternal God. But the verbiage and the dancing relationship continue!

Borrowing some of the language of the saints quoted thus far, God is engaged in a wonderful Divine Dance—interpenetrating, interconnected, consubstantial, coeternal, preexistent, infinitely excellent Three-yet-One. All speak of the relationship which both describes the inner reality of the Godhead—and the only reality by which humans can know or "dance" with the Godhead.

Christian disciples serve a relational, relationship-seeking God, whose very nature and being are the opposite of domination, manipulation, or intimidation; God is Love, Truth, and Humility.[33] Furthermore, God desires to share what He is with His creation, particularly those "created in His image." C. Baxter Kruger relates both the transforming revelation that enlightened his understanding of the ontology of God and the amazing deduction that occurs once this revelation is absorbed:

All along I had been thinking about God the wrong way. All along I had misjudged the very being of God. I had been a blind idiot. God is not some faceless, all-powerful abstraction. God is Father, Son, and Spirit, existing in a passionate and joyous fellowship. The Trinity is not three highly committed religious types sitting around some room in heaven. The Trinity is a circle of shared life, and the life shared is full, not empty, abounding and rich and beautiful, not lonely and sad and boring. The river begins right there, in the fellowship of the Trinity. The great dance is all about the abounding *life* shared by the Father, Son, and Spirit.

And:

It all boils down to three things: First, there is the Trinity and the great dance of life and glory and joy shared by the Father, Son, and Spirit; second there is the incarnation as the act of the Father, Son, and Spirit reaching down, extending the circle, their great dance of life, to us; third, there is our humanity, which is the theatre in which the great dance is played out through the Spirit. *That* is what motherhood and fatherhood are all about. That is what fishing and baseball and playing are all about, and laughter and romance, cookouts and work. They are the very ways the beauty of Father, Son and Spirit, the great dance of the Triune God, the glory, the fellowship, the life are played out in us.[34]

Thus, the Godhead is a circle of life—a life passionate, joyous, rich, and beautiful. That God would extend this circle of dancing to include us is the miracle of the incarnation. It is the heart of His creative love perfectly displayed in humanity's original righteousness. God created humans to dance with Him, even as He danced within Himself. Sadly, the first Adam rebelled, thereby taking on for all humankind an ontology diametrically opposite to the one known at Creation. Ever since the Fall, humans have been bound to operate in an ontology that emanates directly from satan unless and until God's transforming work is accomplished in them.

An outstanding example of satan's ontology operating in humans is the fact that humans are quick to blame God for the fallen condition of all creation. It began in Eden with Adam blaming Eve and Eve blaming the serpent for their disobedience. Blame, a common denominator in all three forms of control, was an immediate result of the Fall.[35] As Jack Hayford, sharing about Kingdom dynamics before the Fall, has said:

> The original order of man's environment on earth must be distinguished from what it became following the impact of man's Fall, the Curse, and the eventual Deluge (Is. 45:18; Rom. 8:20; 2 Pet. 3:4-7). The agricultural, zoological, geological, and meteorological disharmony to which creation became subject must not be attributed to God. The perfect will of God, as founding King of creation, is *not* manifest in the presence of death, disease, discord, and disaster any more than it is manifest in human sin. Our present world does not reflect the kingdom order He originally intended for man's enjoyment on earth, nor does it reflect God's kingdom as it shall ultimately be experienced on this planet. Understanding this, we should be cautious not to attribute to "God's will" or to "acts of God" those characteristics of our world that resulted from the ruin of God's original order by reason of man's Fall.[36]

The devastation wrought by humanity's fall from God's ontology to satan's must not be minimized. In fact, it can't even be fully summarized or verbalized. Every aspect of human nature and of all creation is so greatly distorted as to make immeasurable the distance between what-is-the-present reality and the what-was-and-will-be reality. Only Jesus can bridge the span; only in Him is there hope of restoration. However, in order to better understand the devastating power, distance, darkness, and wickedness at work in the Fall, we must understand the diametric opposite of God's ontology.

The Opposite of True Character

Jesus, speaking *"to those Jews who believed Him"* (John 8:31), said,

> *You are of your father the devil, and the desires of your father you want to do. He was a murderer from the beginning, and does not stand in the truth, because there is no truth in him. When he speaks a lie, he speaks from his own resources* [character], *for he is a liar and the father of it* (John 8:44).

Obviously, belief alone in Jesus does not change human nature and character, or the fact that it is fundamentally the same as satan's. That the *being* of satan is deeply rooted in all humanity is implicit in the theology of the Fall. To understand the essence of the Fall, we must understand the fact that satan's very being was warped as well as the fact that humanity fell into that *distortion*. In assuming satan's image and character, humanity exchanged the dance for deception, truth for lies, and intimacy (nakedness) for guilt and shame (see Gen. 3:1-7).

We have identified domination, intimidation, and manipulation as the manifestations of the murderous, lying ontology of satan. To understand the Good News of Jesus, humans must recognize the availability of grace to restore what was lost—ultimately, the very character, being, and image of God. It is equally important, however, to understand the grotesque condition, the grotesque ontology, in which humans are *by nature* entrapped via the Fall.

While examining the ontology of the Triune God, we have touched on the state of humanity in original righteousness. Next, in an attempt to discover the very "being" of original sin, let us scrutinize the ontology of the most fallen of all, satan. In doing so, we will recognize the current state of humanity in fallen sinfulness.

Chapter Three

THE NATURE OF SATAN

Lucifer—as well as Humpty Dumpty and humanity—had "a great fall." Originally, he was an *"anointed cherub"* (Ezek. 28:14) entrusted with *covering* (protecting) the throne of the Most High God.[1] How did he descend from being "an anointed cherub" to satan, fallen angel and "the father of lies" (see John 8:44)? How did he tumble from guarding God's throne to "eating dust" (see Gen. 3:14)? That's where we will begin our examination of the ontology of satan.

As Gilbert Bilezikian has said, the Bible "very discreetly, almost reluctantly" gives us a glimpse of "the existence of an order of created beings prior to humans."[2] Peering into these passages, we see the very twisting and distorting of lucifer's character as well as the development of intimidation, manipulation, and domination. We see a usurper's attempt to be God, to have sovereignty, authority, and dominion. The results, however, were something opposite and infinitely lower—*control.*

Isaiah 14:12-14 reads:

How you are fallen from heaven, O Lucifer, son of the morning! How you are cut down to the ground, you who weakened the nations! For you have said in your heart: "I will ascend into heaven, I will exalt my throne above the stars of God; I will

*also sit on the mount of the congregation on the farthest sides
of the north; I will ascend above the heights of the clouds, I will
be like the Most High."*

In regard to this pivotal Scripture in Isaiah, several observations
should be made. First, this passage, as well as a passage from Ezekiel
28, speaks of satan in the context of an evil ruler, in this case the
king of Babylon.[3] Many scholars believe this is a device intentionally
inserted in Scripture to reinforce the reality that fallen human behavior
is simply a reflection of satan's ontology. Second, the name *lucifer* or
light bearer,[4] as compared with *satan*, meaning *adversary*,[5] is worthy
of note. Just as God's redemptive and salvific grace changed the name
of Simon to Peter and Abram to Abraham to incorporate the new
character of each, God has changed lucifer's name to accommodate
his new nature. By his own fall, the one who was once the *angel of light*
(and still masquerades as one!)[6] has become *adversary* and *accuser* of
God and humanity!

A third observation to be noted is the fact that lucifer five
times made the declaration "I will." Marilyn Hickey has written the
following regarding these statements and God's response in each case:

> Satan was once as angel called Lucifer, who, in love with
> his own beauty, fell into pride and self-centeredness. His
> rebellion manifests in five "I will" statements addressed
> against God (vv. 13, 14). With five utterances he declares
> that he will take the place of the Most High God. But vv.
> 15-20 reveal the God has the last word, as the Most High
> makes five responses: "Satan, you will 1) be thrown into
> hell; 2) be gazed upon (that is, made a spectacle); 3) be
> talked about (mocked, scorned); 4) be cast out of your
> grave like a carcass; and 5) be alone." God's "last word" on
> Satan is still applicable to any challenge he attempts to bring
> against any of the people of God.[7]

The five "I will" statements display the "pride and self-
centeredness" that provoked lucifer's fall. Even more important to
note, however, is the fact that lucifer's failure is both illuminated and
sealed by God's response.

This book addresses the fact that control, through domination, intimidation, and manipulation, is the product of trying to be like God. In agreement with Scripture, the perpetrator has been identified, satan, and by ontological duplication, fallen humanity. Just as pride (self-centeredness) is always the root of trying to be God, control is always its expression. The king of Babylon acted under this delusion as a *representative* of all fallen humanity, and as a *reflection* of the devil. In similar fashion, the king of Tyre personified satan as well as all sinful humanity. Again, a passage with several levels of meaning emerges:

Moreover, the word of the Lord came to me, saying, "Son of man, take up a lamentation for the king of Tyre, and say to him, 'Thus says the Lord God; you were the seal of perfection, full of wisdom and perfect in beauty. You were in Eden, the garden of God; every precious stone was your covering; the sardius, topaz, and diamond, beryl, onyx, and jasper, sapphire, turquoise, and emerald with gold. The workmanship of your timbrels and pipes was prepared for you on the day you were created. You were the anointed cherub who covers; I established you; you were on the holy mountain of God; you walked back and forth in the midst of fiery stones. You were perfect in your ways from the day you were created, till iniquity was found in you. By the abundance of your trading you became filled with violence within, and you sinned; therefore I cast you as a profane thing out of the mountain of God; and I destroyed you, O covering cherub, from the midst of the fiery stones. Your heart was lifted up because of your beauty; you corrupted your wisdom for the sake of your splendor; I cast you to the ground, I laid you before kings, that they might gaze at you. You defiled your sanctuaries by the multitude of your iniquities, by the iniquity of your trading; therefore I brought fire from your midst; it devoured you, and I turned you to ashes upon the earth in the sight of all who saw you. All who knew you among the peoples are astonished at you; you have become a horror, and shall be no more forever" (Ezekiel 28:11-19).

The king of Tyre, like Adam and satan before him, chose rebellion over relationship, resulting in the distortion of life as well as the distortion of self. By referencing both satan and the king of Tyre in the same passage, God's Word was simply layering the passage to show that the same old fallen nature manifests, with startling similarity, over and over again. It is as if we humans share the basic core of our character with each other and satan!

The Ezekiel passage also seems to describe Lucifer's role and character prior to his fall. Some scholars suggest that *"timbrels and pipes"* (v. 13) indicates that satan was once the worship leader of Heaven.[8] In addition, the stones seem to depict a priestly ephod (see Exodus 28), suggesting the once-priestly position of satan/Adam/the king of Tyre.[9]

Of further interest is a comparison between the Exodus 28 passage and the description of the perfected Bride of Christ, the New Jerusalem, in Revelation 21:9–22:5. Adorned with precious stones, this Bride (this city) will rule and reign in priestly authority with the Lamb forever. Might she, the Church, not be the new and everlasting worship leader—the redeemed, perfected, and permanent replacement for lucifer? Certainly, her stones represent apostolic authority.[10] In any case, a perfected human ontology will flawlessly reflect God in His perichoretic relationship, and will therefore be the diametric opposite of satan and his controlling character, as evidenced in the *anti-Trinity*[11] activities of domination, intimidation, and manipulation.

Most interestingly, the Ezekiel 28 passage gives us a glimpse into the root pride and arrogance that birthed domination, intimidation, and manipulation in satan, and by later extension, in all humanity. Verse 16 states: *"By the abundance of your trading you became filled with violence within...."* Thus, wealth and the acquisition of it led to "violence," an indication of the birth of *domination*. Domination is always accomplished by passive—or not so passive—aggression and violence. This thought continues in verse 17: *"...You corrupted your wisdom for the sake of your splendor...."* Satan's splendor led to "corrupt wisdom," a description of the birth of *manipulation*. Manipulation involves a corrupting of truth to gain control, often in a subtle, behind-the-scenes fashion. The earlier part of verse 17 depicts the birth of intimidation: *"Your heart was lifted up because of your beauty...."* Satan's beauty led to a "prideful heart," which describes the origin of *intimidation*. It is this pride, often covering deep insecurity, that prompts intimidation. Obviously, the perpetuation of these three characteristics was the basis of satan's corruption and of his ontological fall, replacing the wealth (provision), splendor, and beauty that were satan's very nature in God's original creative love. To think that wealth, beauty, and splendor, all reflective of God's Self-being, could be so horribly reduced to domination, manipulation, and intimidation is indicative of the depth, depravity, and horror of the *original fall:* satan's.

The pattern established in the beginning will be repeated in the end times. An unholy trinity will become especially apparent in the last of the last days (see Rev. 16:13). Clearly, the beast (representing political and military power and the leader wielding it)[12] is a manifestation of manipulation. The dragon (satan) manifests domination as part of this perverse trinity. The false prophet (both a person and religious system)[13] manifests intimidation, empowering religiosity. In something akin to bookends, satan's warped ontology is depicted "in the beginning" and in the very end. Satan, if nothing else, is predictable.

While the references in Isaiah and Ezekiel give a glimpse into how and why lucifer became satan and what that fall encompassed (and encompasses), the one in Revelation indicates what will soon become painfully obvious—things satan will yet attempt before his *final fall.* Passages throughout Scripture reveal what satan was (and is) ontologically and, central to this project, how human ontology so closely mimics his. In fact, it has been noted that "there are only four chapters in the Bible where satan is not present, the first two and the last two. The Bible begins and ends with him out of existence. But between Genesis 3 and Revelation 20 he is a factor to be reckoned with."[14]

A Snake Cannot Be Disguised

Genesis 3:1-7 gives us a remarkable image of satan after his fall, even as it explains humanity's Fall by portraying mankind as "dressed" in satan's fallen ontology. In the first five verses we read:

Now the serpent was more cunning than any beast of the field which the Lord God had made. And he said to the woman, "Has God indeed said, 'You shall not eat of every tree of the garden'?" And the woman said to the serpent, "We may eat the fruit of the trees of the garden; but of the fruit of the tree which is in the midst of the garden, God has said, 'You shall not eat it, nor shall you touch it, lest you die.'" Then the serpent said to the woman, "You shall not surely die. For God knows that in the day you eat of it your eyes will be opened, and you will be like God, knowing good and evil" (Genesis 3:1-5).

Perhaps the first thing to cite is the manifestation of satan as a serpent. "In Hebrew, the word *serpent* is a pun for 'one who practices divination,' indicating efforts to access the divine will for self-advantage"[15] Obviously, satan's ontological craving for power could not be hidden. A snake can neither be hidden nor disguised. Satan's nature betrayed him: he looked like what he had become.

Adam and Eve had every reason to recognize and deal with this snake in the grass. According to *The International Bible Commentary*, the temptation came "not from a superior being, but from an inferior, over whom the woman should have exercised dominion."[16] Adam, however, was guilty of the greater fault. God had entrusted him with the responsibility and authority to "tend and keep," or "work and protect" The Garden (see Gen. 2:15). Protect from what? From lucifer, whose grotesque snakelike character could not be hidden! Adam's failure to protect Eve and The Garden, along with Eve's failure to exercise dominion, led to the horrific exchange of dominion for control. It should never be forgotten that, in original righteousness, humanity had perfect dominion over satan. More importantly for us, it should never be forgotten that, in Christ, we have "authority to trample on serpents and scorpions, and over all the power of the enemy, with nothing being able to hurt us (see Luke 10:19) unless we fail to exercise the authority given to us. Obviously, Adam and Eve failed to exercise the protective dominion authority given them, to their (and our) great harm.

Dominion Versus Domination

Dominion, given by the Father, Son, and Holy Spirit at Creation, was (and is) the absolute opposite of control. Dominion flows from greater authority; control, from a lack of authority, or from a vain attempt to usurp authority. True to His perfect ontology, God, the ultimate Authority, freely and fully shared His authority with His highest creation, humanity. He gave us dominion! However, we should never confuse *dominion* with *domination!* Domination, one of the three manifestations of control, flows from self-appointed authority. Along with manipulation and intimidation, it is diametrically opposite to the beautiful flow of perfect authority/dominion given to humankind "in the beginning." Since satan had no authority to take or give dominion, he had to deceive our first two ancestors into relinquishing their dominion in exchange for pathetic control. What a horrible fall!

Now, Back to Satan

The third chapter of Genesis gives further insight into the character of satan. We get a glimpse of his false-trinitarian nature as we identify the three temptations he employed. When he said to Eve, *"You will not surely die"* (Gen. 3:4), he, operating in the realm of domination, was tempting Eve from a *physical* standpoint.[17] On the other hand, he was operating in the realm of manipulation and tempting Eve from an *emotional* standpoint when he asked the not-so-subtle question in Genesis 3:1, *"Has God indeed said, 'You shall not eat of every tree of the garden'?"*[18] Then, following this sneaky attack on the character of God, satan enticed (intimidated) Eve's *spiritual* being[19] saying, *"You will be like God"* (Gen. 3:5). Thus, in this passage, we see satan's ontology exposed as he dominated, manipulated, and intimidated Eve in a trinity of attacks focused on her triune[20] nature. Had Eve operated in her God-given dominion, or had Adam protected her from the snake in the first place, all history would be different! Sadly, however, they failed; and we all fell.

Genesis 3:6 is pivotal to this book, because it records the "irresistible"[21] transfer of ontology from satan to Eve and Adam. The verse says: *"So when the woman saw that the tree was **good for food,** that it was **pleasant to the eyes,** and a tree desirable to **make one wise,** she took of its fruit and ate. She also gave to her husband with her, and he ate."*

In Eve's (and Adam's) response to this *tripartite* temptation, we see the trinity of rebellion, physical, emotional (soulish), and spiritual. They responded in a *dominating* way, expressing that the "tree was good for food"; in a *manipulating* way, as they noticed that it was "pleasant to the eyes;" and in an *intimidating* way, noting that the tree was "desirable to make one wise." What had before been only satan's ontological perversion (and that of the other fallen angels) was now Eve and Adam's. They suddenly thought like him, and their new ontological "knowledge" brought embarrassment and shame, not God-like wisdom.[22]

Dressing in the Wrong Tree

What transpires next in Scripture is an amazing picture of this ontological transfer: *"Then the eyes of both of them were opened, and they knew that they were naked; and they sewed fig leaves together and made themselves coverings"* (Gen. 3:7). According to ancient Jewish thought and tradition, the tree of the knowledge of good and evil was a fig tree,[23] and the leaves sewn together following the eating of the fruit were those plucked from the same tree.[24] Dressing in the "tree of the knowledge of good and evil," Adam and Eve actually "put on" that to which they had just succumbed. Adam and Eve's dressing themselves depicts the very nature of rebellion, of satan's ontology. The fact that God redressed them in *"tunics of skin"* (Gen. 3:21) greatly reinforces this concept. As Charles Simpson has stated:

> The covenant love of God required that innocent animals be sacrificed to provide garments of skin as a covering for Adam and Eve. This early foreshadowing of substitutionary atonement points toward the necessity of judgment upon

the innocent to provide a covering for the guilty. Adam and Eve made a vain attempt to cover themselves with their own efforts by sewing together fig leaves. However, God's order provided covering by means of a sacrifice. Under the New Covenant, we are required to be clothed with Christ rather than with our good works.[25]

The ontological picture is stunning. Adam and Eve, as well as all their fallen children, *dress* in what is easily and naturally at hand—satan's ontology. God, on the other hand, desires to dress us in the clothing of an innocent substitute; He desires to clothe us with His righteous ontology in the blood and Body of Christ Jesus. God provides what humanity, in our fallen ontology, cannot even comprehend, much less supply—an Innocent Substitute. This "Tunic of Life" undoes in humanity what cannot otherwise be undone, satan's nature and character which clothes humanity by virtue of the Fall. Christ came to remove the fig leaves of our fallen nature, and to dress His disciples in His own character. On their own, humans will naturally attempt to fix the problem themselves, by religious effort or "good works."[26] This attempt correlates religiosity with control, something like two sides of the same fallen, satanic, ontological *fig leaf.*

Therefore, it should come as no surprise that Jesus enacted His parable about the fruitless religiousness of Israel with the cursing of a *fig tree* (see Matt. 21:18-19). Religiousness can look good from afar and be inviting from a distance, but with closer inspection it is obviously only outward show. Fig leaves of good works are cursedly superficial to those hungry for real fruit. It made Jesus weep to see His beloved people Israel (still!) clothed in nothing but fig leaves even with the Tunic Himself in her midst!

In Luke 4:1-13, we see satan's very predictable *modus operandi* displayed again, this time with and to the Second Adam. Satan's first temptation of Christ is recorded in Luke 4:1-4:

> *Then Jesus, being filled with the Holy Spirit, returned from the Jordan and was led by the Spirit into the wilderness, being tempted for forty days by the devil. And in those days He*

ate nothing, and afterward, when they had ended, He was hungry. And the devil said to Him, "If You are the Son of God, command this stone to become bread." But Jesus answered him, saying, "It is written, 'Man shall not live by bread alone, but by every word of God.'"

Speaking from his own ontological trait of domination, satan attempted to lure Jesus, hungry and fully human, with an offer of food. Domination is usually manifested in the *physical realm*. Yet, responding from His own ontology, Jesus blocked the domination by focusing on the life that flows from feasting on the Godhead relationally.[27] Domination was blocked by submitted relationship as Jesus resisted physical temptation.

The second temptation of Christ is recorded in Luke 4:5-8:

Then the devil, taking Him up on a high mountain, showed Him all the kingdoms of the world in a moment of time. And the devil said to Him, "All this authority I will give You, and their glory; for this has been delivered to me, and I give it to whomever I wish. Therefore, if You will worship before me, all will be Yours." And Jesus answered and said to him, "Get behind Me, Satan! For it is written, 'You shall worship the Lord your God, and Him only you shall serve.'"

Jesus' second temptation in the wilderness depicts the second method of control, manipulation. Satan offered to give Jesus what He had come for (the peoples and nations), without His having to pay the price of obedience. Satan assumed he could tempt Jesus in the *soulish realm*; yet, true to His very being, Jesus refused to be manipulated. He insisted on nothing less than the "dance" of perfect relationship within the Godhead. Motivated by a perfect resolve to obediently worship and serve, again a picture of a submitted "dancing" relationship,[28] Jesus stymied satan's manipulative attempt to lure Him to sin. The mind, will, and emotions (soul) are an easy target for manipulation; obedient relationship with God, a sure defense.

As one would expect, the third temptation satan offered Jesus depicts the third means of control, intimidation:

Then he brought Him to Jerusalem, set Him on the pinnacle of the temple, and said to Him, "If You are the Son of God, throw Yourself down from here. For it is written: 'He shall give His angels charge over you, to keep you,' and, 'In their hands they shall bear you up, lest you dash your foot against a stone.'" And Jesus answered and said to him, "It has been said, 'You shall not tempt the Lord your God'" (Luke 4:9-12).

Attacking Jesus in the *spiritual realm*, satan cajoled Jesus, in effect saying, "You are God, and you deserve to be treated as such. Now go show your stuff!" Henry Nouwen called this the "temptation to be powerful."[29] However, the One who knows perfect, humble relationship foiled satan's attempt to control by intimidation.

Both *The Nelson Study Bible* and the *New Spirit Filled Life Bible* contain a table at the bottom of the page at Luke 4 which compares the first Adam with the Second. Because the table corroborates material compiled for this project, it is reproduced here.[30]

TEMPTATION: The Two Adams Contrasted (4:1,2)		
Both Adam and Christ faced three aspects of temptation. Adam yielded, bringing upon humankind sin and death. Christ resisted, resulting in justification and life.		
1 John 2:16	Genesis 3:6 First Adam	Luke 4:1-13 Second Adam—Christ
"the lust of the flesh"	"the tree was good for food"	"command this stone to become bread"
"the lust of the eyes"	"it was pleasant to the eyes"	"the devil...showed Him all the kingdoms"
"the pride of life"	"a tree desirable to make one wise"	"throw Yourself down from here"

Now, expanded with a focus on control, as prepared by this researcher:

Control Type	Final Temptation Matt. 26:36-46	Works of Flesh Gal. 5:16-24	The World 1 John 2:16	False Teachers Jude 11	In the Church Rev. 2-3	Final Battle Rev. 16:13
Domination	"This cup"…	"selfish ambition"	"the lust of the flesh"	"the way of Cain"	"doctrine of the Nicolaitans"	the dragon (satan)
Manipulation	"This cup"…	"discord dissentions, factions"	"the lust of the eyes"	"the error of Balaam"	"doctrine of Balaam"	the beast (antichrist)
Intimidation	"This cup"…	"fits of rage; hatred"	"the pride of life"	"The rebellion of Korah"	"That woman Jezebel…a prophetess"	the false prophet

And continued...

The pattern, repeated and predictable, is nonetheless stunningly significant as the impact of satanic ontology is seen across the pages of Scripture and the span of time. Especially significant for disciples in the Church Age is the recognition of the tripartite temptations manifest in the false trinity of domination, intimidation, and manipulation so apparent in *"the world"* (1 John 2:16); in "false teachers" within the Church (see Jude 11); and in control-ism in the Church (see Rev. 2-3). Obviously, whether manifest through teachers and leaders or through any other person in the Body, control is sin. It is the visible essence of temptation, emanating from the fallen realm of the evil world. Of the wrong ontology, it is the opposite of the perichoretic (dancing) reality of perfect relationship. In a word, it is *satan*.

Several other New Testament Scriptures help to delineate the ontological makeup of satan, as well as set the priorities for those who follow Christ Jesus. In Luke 10:17-20, Scripture records Jesus' response to the joy of the 70 concerning the authority they experienced over the demonic. The passage reads:

> *Then the seventy returned with joy, saying, "Lord, even the demons are subject to us in Your name." And He said to them, "I saw satan fall like lightning from heaven. Behold, I give you the authority to trample on serpents and scorpions, and over all the power of the enemy, and nothing shall by any means hurt you. Nevertheless do not rejoice in this, that the spirits are subject to you, but rather rejoice because your names are written in heaven."*

As well as relating an interesting comparison between "serpents and scorpions" and demonic powers,[31] this passage may allude to satan's original fall,[32] to his "present and ultimate" defeat through the cross,[33] and to fallen man's temptation to be prideful.[34] However, the most interesting and most important inference is that Jesus emphasized the relational reality of heavenly life over authority over demons.[35] More simply said, our relationship with the Lord should be our highest goal, not the authority over evil that comes with that relationship. Our focus should be "dancing" with God!

Satan, Control, and the Enemies of Israel

Satan's conflict with Israel, both physical and spiritual Israel, is well seen in the tables and the Scriptures thus far mentioned. His hatred for her is overwhelming, and his war against her, always waged with the weapons of control, will continue until Messiah returns. The sheer number of times satanic control is manifest against Israel in the pages of Scripture could fill up several more tables, and indeed, books. A few more examples are helpful, however, in recognizing the repeated pattern.

In the fourth chapter of Ezra, a group of people described as *"the adversaries of Judah"* (v. 1) use all three methods of control to attempt to halt the reconstruction of the Temple over a period of several years. Manipulation was the method of choice first attempted by the adversaries. Feigning a desire to help with the construction, the enemy came to Zerubbabel, offering assistance (see Ezra 4:2). Zerubbabel wisely rejected their manipulations. With manipulation failing, the same group resorted to intimidation, hiring *"counselors against them to frustrate their purpose all the days of Cyrus king of Persia"* (Ezra 4:5). Again, their efforts failed. Domination, in the form of a letter to King Artaxerxes followed, and was temporarily successful in stopping progress of the project (see Ezra 4:7-24). Ultimately, of course, control failed and God prevailed: The Temple was rebuilt.

Another example comes from the pages of Nehemiah. Predictably, there were three primary adversaries to Nehemiah as he led Israel in the rebuilding of Jerusalem's walls: Sanballet, Tobiah, and Geshem. They conspired together to halt the construction, manifesting aspects of control individually and collectively. Domination manifested as the three adversaries, full of despising hatred and indignant laughter, accused Nehemiah and the nation of rebellion (see Neh. 2:19). Sanballet in particular seemed to operate as a dominator. Intimidation manifested in the threats of imminent and overwhelming attack issued by the enemies as the wall construction progressed (see Neh. 4:7-8). The fact that they were *"very angry"* (vs. 7) speaks of intimidation. Geshem probably manifested intimidation the most clearly of the three. Manipulation is clearly seen in the invitation to come and meet on the plain of Ono, a ploy Nehemiah saw through just as clearly (see Neh. 6:2). A dominating and intimidating letter was then sent (see Neh. 6:5-9), followed by a very devious form of manipulation as a "secret informer" tried to lure Nehemiah into the temple (see Neh. 6:10-19). Tobiah was particularly involved in these acts of manipulation. In all, the enemies of Nehemiah and the people attempted seven times to stop the construction, but in each case the three methods of control and the three controlling leaders were defeated by the God of Nehemiah.

One final example should suffice in the discussion of Israel's enemies and their use of control. Occasionally, a person will surface who is an absolute *master* of their trade. Queen Jezebel certainly exemplifies a *master intimidator*, as does the giant Goliath. Pharaoh pictures well a *master dominator*. His hard-hearted attempts to squash Moses and Israel clearly depict rock-crushing domination. The most interesting picture of a master of their trade, however, is of Antiochus IV, who will surely go down as one of the "greatest" *master manipulators* of all time.

Daniel prophesied about Antiochus, describing him using terms such as "intrigue" (see Dan. 11:21), "flattery" (see Dan. 11:32), and "slipperiness" (see Dan. 11:34; synonym for *flattery* and *intrigue*) to illustrate his masterful use of manipulation. Daniel 11 gives a sobering description of the anti-Christ Antiochus, as well as the ultimate antichrist, who will, of course, manifest manipulation on an even more masterful level. Describing Antiochus as a *"vile person"* (Dan. 11:21) who exalts himself above all others (see Dan. 11:37), Daniel describes for us in chilling detail the controlling heart of one who will turn from anyone, even God, and turn toward anything, especially religiousness, to manipulate his way into ultimate power.

Indeed, Israel has been fighting against *control* from without and within for her entire existence, and the war, unfortunately, is still raging. The god of *control*, satan, will attempt to destroy Israel after the flesh and after the spirit one last time in a terrifying triune fashion. Ironically, this last-gasp effort to control Israel will instead result in her salvation and in her unification as Judah and Ephraim, Jew and Greek, nation and Church, physical and spiritual, are united together forever in our Messiah!

Overcoming Satan's Control

Revelation 12:7-12 expands additional insight into satan's fall and his methods of attack directed against humanity. The passage states:

> *And war broke out in heaven: Michael and his angels fought with the dragon; and the dragon and his angels fought, but they did not prevail, nor was a place found for them in heaven any longer. So the great dragon was cast out, that serpent of old, called the devil and satan, who deceives the whole world; he was cast to the earth, and his angels were cast out with him. Then I heard a loud voice saying in heaven, "Now salvation, and strength, and the kingdom of our God, and the power of His Christ have come, for the accuser of our brethren, who accused them before our God day and night, has been cast down. And they overcame him by the blood of the Lamb and by the word of their testimony, and they did not love their lives to the death. Therefore rejoice, O heavens, and you who dwell in them! Woe to the inhabitants of the earth and the sea! For the devil has come down to you, having great wrath, because he knows that he has a short time."*

Jack W. Hayford makes the point that this passage, viewed through the lens of various interpretive systems, has brought division in the Body concerning the timing within redemptive history.[36] Regardless of the interpretive system, the passage makes clear that satan—"that serpent of old," the devil, the "accuser of our brethren," and the dragon—are all one and the same. Further, the text provides legitimacy in terms of referring to satan as "he," a person (fallen angel), not simply a concept. The text presents a picture of "age-long warfare,"[37] best understood as a sweeping panorama encapsulating a vast chronology into a few short verses.

Most interesting, however, is the tripartite description of those who, in Jesus, "overcome" satan and his demonic throng. The text states that *"They overcame him* [satan] *by the blood of the Lamb and by the word of their testimony, and they did not love their lives to the death"* (Rev. 12:11). In the context of this project, these three points can be made:

Control Type	Realm of Attack	Satan's Fall *Ezek. 28:16-17*	First Temptation *Gen. 3:1-5*	Transfer: *Gen. 3:6-7*	Temptation of Christ *Luke 4:1-13*
Domination	Physical (Body)	Wealth—"filled with violence"	"You will not surely die"	"The tree was good for food"	"Command this stone to become bread"
Manipulation	Emotional (Soul)	Corrupt wisdom—"your splendor"	"Has God indeed said...?"	"It was pleasant to the eyes"	"The devil... showed Him all the kingdoms"
Intimidation	Spiritual (Spirit)	Heart pride— "your beauty"	"You will be like God"	"A tree desirable to make one wise"	"Throw Yourself down from here"

1. Satan cannot *manipulate* brethren who know who they are and discern the acceptance they have in and by the blood of Jesus. In other words, the blood defeats the accuser's power in the emotional or soulish realm.[38]

2. Satan cannot *intimidate* brethren who possess a testimony by the power of the Word. The devil's capacity to intimidate is lost upon believers who know and testify to greater power. In other words, the *word of testimony* brings victory over satan in his attempts to attack Christians through their spiritual being.[39]

3. Satan cannot *dominate* those who love Jesus more than life itself; who have "crucified the flesh," and no longer fear death. In other words, a fearless dying-to-self eliminates satan's ability to provoke fear in the physical or bodily realm.[40]

"Overcoming Christianity," therefore, embodies faith that destroys satan's ability to control and simultaneously crucifies the control nature within the believer.

Overcoming Rock/Paper/Scissors

Let's extend the above discussion to our example of the game Rock/Paper/Scissors. Again, the passage states:

"And they overcame him [satan] *by the blood of the Lamb and by the word of their testimony, and they did not love their lives to the death"* (Revelation 12:11).

Applying the above notations to this passage, let us note:

1. Since satan cannot manipulate brethren who know who they are and discern the acceptance they have in and by the blood of Jesus, then the blood routs paper!

2. Since satan cannot intimidate brethren who possess a testimony by the power of the Word, then our testimonies to the Word's glory defeats scissors!

3. Since satan cannot *dominate* those who love Jesus more than life itself, who have "crucified the flesh" and no longer fear death, then loving Jesus more than life crushes rock!

Clearly, the authority Jesus gives His followers overcomes satan's ploys of control: manipulation, intimidation, and domination. Furthermore, Christians should never resort to satan's techniques in daily living and never stoop to playing the game of Rock/Paper/Scissors. When Jesus' blood, Word, and love are introduced, the game of control is overcome by the *Way of Life*. Jesus is the only way to quit playing the control game; He is the only way to overcome satan's nature found naturally in us; He allows us to quit playing God, quit playing control, and quit playing games in relationships!

Meet Some Overcomers

Peter readily comes to mind as an "overcomer." At first, he knew how to play Rock/Paper/Scissors. Being a manipulator, he tended to throw "paper," and satan certainly knew how to play on this weakness in his soul. Peter wanted to build three tabernacles on the Mount of Transfiguration (see Matt. 17:4). He even tried to dissuade Jesus from going to the cross (see Matt. 16:21-23). However, after Jesus went to the cross and then came back and *breathed* on the disciples, the game was over for Peter. Any second thoughts were put to rest on the shore of the Sea of Galilee (see John 21). Satan lost power over Peter; tradition holds that he went to a cross rather than succumb to satan's manipulation, domination, and intimidation. By the "blood of the Lamb," Peter overcame satan's manipulations and was set free of his own manipulative propensities.

James (half-brother to Jesus) was also an overcomer. Having once doubted Jesus' authenticity (see John 7:3-5), he became a leader in the early Church (see Acts 12:17; 15:13ff; 21:18). Obviously, Jesus' post-resurrection appearance to him (see 1 Cor. 15:7), had made him a believer and an overcomer who could no longer be intimidated by attacks against his spiritual being. By the "word of his testimony," James overcame satan's intimidations and was liberated from his own tendency to intimidate others.

A list of overcomers, of course, would not be complete without naming Paul. Talk about the game of control, he even participated in the killing of Christians in the *game*. However, through repeated physical torture and pain, Paul came to the end of himself and his resources.[41] He became an overcomer, no longer threatened by physical abuse, torture, a thorn in the flesh, or death itself (see 1 Cor. 15:54-55). Because Paul did not love his physical life, even unto death, satan lost his power to attack Paul, especially in the physical realm. By "not loving life, even unto death," Paul overcame satan's dominations and was essentially freed from his prior inclination to dominate others.

Down through the ages, "overcoming disciples" like those seen in the New Testament have gained victory over satan and over the fallen ontological nature inherited from him. As Jesus explained concerning Himself in John 14:30, satan has no power over those in whom satan is unable to establish a "foothold"[42] or place of attack in a believer's life. This is overcoming Christianity: when, by God's grace the places of vulnerability within a person's spirit, soul, and body are closed to satan, *and* the bent toward controlling others is surrendered.

The table on the facing page outlines the transformations of Peter, James, and Paul.

The examples (Simon/Peter, skeptic James/apostle James, and Saul/Paul) demonstrate the fact that relationship with God closes the doors of access to satan's temptations in a believer. Furthermore, an intimate relationship with God causes a transformation in the believer that helps them stop playing the satanic game of control. Talk about a Divine Dance! Doors are closed, lives are changed, and game-playing ceases.

Scripture gives other insights into satan's ontology. We see his characteristics in his actions; he *"entered Judas"* (Luke 22:3) and asked "to sift" Peter (see Luke 22:31); he deceives and ensnares (see 2 Cor. 11:3-5; 1 Tim. 3:6-7; Rev. 20:7-8); he *"transforms himself into an angel of light"* (2 Cor. 11:14); he *"walks about like a roaring lion, seeking whom he may devour"* (1 Pet. 5:8). On the other hand, satan can be overcome by the resistance of believers (see James 4:7 and 1 Pet. 5:9); he can be put underfoot by believers (see Rom. 16:20).

Control Type	Unredeemed Examples	Most Valued:	Key Scriptures	Changed by:	Redeemed by Grace:	New Value:	Perfected By:
Domination	Saul (Religiously bound)	Winning	Acts 9:1-30	Love	Paul (Apostle to the Greeks)	Finishing	"Love thy enemies" Matt. 5:44
Manipulation	Simon "Hear Me"	Being Accepted	Matt. 16:13-23; John 21	Truth	Peter "Little rock"	Being Faithful	"made perfect in one" John 17:23
Intimidation	James, unbelieving half-brother to Jesus in the flesh	Being Right	John 7:3-4; 1 Cor. 15:7	Humility	James, Apostle: Full-brother to Jesus by the Spirit	Being Godly	"a perfect man, able to bridle" James 3:2

Perhaps nothing clarifies satan's ontology more than his various names: *"Beelzebub, the prince of demons"* (Matt. 12:24 NIV); the *"evil one"* (Matt. 6:13); *"god of this age"* (2 Cor. 4:4); *"murderer"* and *"father of lies"* (John 8:44 NIV); *"prince of the power of the air"* (Eph. 2:2); "ruler of darkness" (see Eph. 6:12); *"ruler of this world"* (John 14:30); and *"wicked one"* (Matt. 13:19).

Clearly, as revealed in Scripture, satan is both powerful and dangerous; however, he is a defeated foe through the finished work of the cross. Dressed in the armor of Jesus, disciples can stand against all his wiles (see Eph. 6:10-18). Revelation 12:11 gives the means of being an overcomer: *"And they overcame him by the blood of the Lamb and by the word of their testimony, and they did not love their lives to the death."*

Satan—Control Freak? Yes. Equal to God? No Way!

A scriptural review of satan's character and being demonstrates that lucifer fell from his angelic standing into a demonic state; and, manifesting the same ontological traits that brought about his own fall, he seduced Adam and Eve to fall from a sinless to a sinful condition. Pride, self-reliance, and rebellion define the motivations leading to his fall, but domination, manipulation, and intimidation best describe the manifestations of that fall.

Satan, in his very *being,* is the antithesis of the Triune God, manifesting the diametrical opposite of God's perfect perichoretic (dancing) existence with an anti-Trinitarian expression flaunting and belittling God's greatness. But this conflict is no battle between equals. Satan is a created being. Furthermore, he continues to exist only at the will of his Creator, and only with limited power. He may wield control, but not dominion. Although he has usurped some authority, he will never have ultimate authority. Here is the kicker: He can't *dance!*

Although satan manifests a triune control nature, he is not a triune being, just a solo-being wannabe. He purposed in his heart to be *"like the most High"* (Isa. 14:14); but he fell *"like lightening from heaven"* (Luke 10:18). In his corrupted state, he enticed Adam and Eve into thinking they could be "like God." Instead, Adam and Eve took on satan's ontology, forfeiting their original righteousness. Through perverse influence, satan has twisted and warped all of creation, especially humanity. The purpose for displaying his flawed and failed nature in this project has been to show that it was the very corruption of satan that humanity "fell for" and "dressed in" in Genesis 3.

Chapter Four

THE FALL AND RISE
OF HUMAN NATURE

Paul concludes his first letter to the church at Thessalonica with a prayer that provides a great starting place for discussing the ontological makeup of human beings, and the power (grace) available to restore us to right relationship with God. The passage reads, *"Now may the God of peace Himself sanctify you completely; and may your whole spirit, soul, and body be preserved blameless at the coming of our Lord Jesus Christ"* (1 Thess. 5:23).

First, let's celebrate together that we serve a "God of peace" who came to make peace with you and me and all of His fallen creation! Next, we should shout for joy that He has come to sanctify us (set us apart) completely and entirely, and in the here and now, not just in the sweet by and by. But how is that possible? To understand the full implications of this prayer, we must understand the triune nature of humanity: spirit, soul, and body.

We humans were created in the image of our Triune God, and that includes a triune makeup in our very being. We are spirit (pneuma), soul (psuche), and body (soma). In original righteousness, the perfect relationship of these three with one another was a beautiful reflection of the perfect relationship within the Holy Trinity, allowing a perfect relationship with Him. Just as He is truly One God, Adam and Eve were, originally, truly one with God, each other, and within themselves. Our "oneness" was tragically broken in the Fall, and we have been at war with ourselves (not to mention each other!) ever since.

The first two chapters of Genesis give us glimpses into this reality. The human spirit is that part of us—male and female—that was created to inhale the breath of God (see Gen. 1:27; 2:7). God created the human body out of the "dust of the ground" and combined body with spirit, "breathing" (spiriting) life into His creation. This act resulted in the fact that "man became a living soul" (see Gen. 2:7). The soul is the seat of mind, will, and emotions. Thus, God made three one, and all was truly good.

One way to better comprehend the three-in-oneness of humanity is to understand that the human spirit is the seat of God-consciousness, the soul is the seat of self-consciousness, and the body is the seat of world-consciousness.[1] In the beginning, self- and world-consciousness were perfectly aligned with God-consciousness. In the beginning, we "danced" with God!

Another help is to remember that humankind, all that we are, was created in the image of God. Our human spirit was created to commune perfectly with God the Holy Spirit. Our soul was created to commune perfectly with God the Father, and our body was created to commune perfectly with God the Son, Three to three, but perfectly One to one.

This three-in-one being, God's highest creation, originally enjoyed perfect life, in a perfect garden, and in perfect harmony. With *spirit* breathing in perfect relationship with God, *soul* (mind, will, and emotions) effortlessly basking in perfect union, and *body* perfectly full of the glory of the Son, life was fully alive. There was no death, no disease, no disagreement, no conflict, no pain, no stress, and no fear. Just spirit, soul, and body fully embraced in each other, completely indivisible, fully *one* and fully alive in the One who made them!

We must be careful, however, never to make the mistake of thinking that being God's highest creation somehow made humanity divine. God made us perfectly, but He still *made* us. He is God, and we are not! Satan is still trying to tell people they can be "like God," disseminating the lie through all the senseless books about humans somehow being little gods, or having the divine nature *separate from Him*, or growing up to be god, or populating a world as a god (with plenty of pretty and mindless goddesses around). All are rooted in the Fall and in satan's pathetic delusions of grandeur. Let it be remembered that God created humans to relate with Him, the One and only Eternal God, with perfect ease: He as God, and humans as His crowning creation.

Let it also be remembered that this perfect triune package comes with the indescribable gift of free will. Therefore, the relationship with God is a matter of choice, something to be embraced, not something forced upon humanity. God is love, and free will is necessary for true love to operate. Control is a violation of free will. Control is the attempt to override and direct it by intimidation, manipulation, or domination. Control, the awful warping of free will, is the bait to draw wrong decisions from free will. God would not go there; however, by giving free will, He chose to allow His creation to "go there" if they were stupid enough to throw away everything, even the perfect operation of their free will! Lucifer, not triune in being but endowed with free will, led the way. Humanity, in triune splendor, should have known better.

What happened next is no secret: "Stupid" prevailed, and perfect everything gave way to the control-filled mess we now live in. Trying to be "like God," Adam and Eve lost, for themselves and for all humanity, the dominion God had granted His highest creation. Satan, however, would not have the last word! There in The Garden, God set in action His plan to rescue humanity from satan's clutches.

Despite satan's lie to Eve that they would not die if they ate the fruit of the forbidden tree (see Gen. 3:4), God, true to His Word, did cause Adam's and Eve's death the very day they disobeyed. In the face of an extreme fall, God acted in an extreme way: He "closed off" the human spirit; it became dead through sin (see Eph. 2:1-3). Had He not done so, Adam and Eve, and all their posterity, would have been totally and hopelessly owned by the control freak of hell. God replaced the fig leaves with "coats of skin," foreshadowing the means by which their "nakedness" would be covered. Because He would not allow the human spirit to be trapped eternally in the worship of a fallen angel, He shut off the spirit to the enemy—and to Himself.[2]

Genesis 3:22-24 pictures this "closing off" of the human spirit. God, because He could not bear the thought of His highest creation living forever in total and absolute bondage to satan, drove Adam and Eve out of The Garden, placing guards at the door. He sealed the spirit; and humans became, in all reality, bipartite beings.

Now, with the soul in charge and the body full of death, humanity began life under new ownership. Control replaced *dominion* because the soul, without the spirit, cannot operate in dominion. Dominion requires *breath*—from God's Spirit into a human spirit. To be in authority, one must be "under Authority," connected and submitted to the Source of Life. However, that was no longer possible, thanks to God's amazing grace in the face of unspeakable rebellion. It was pure love that closed down the human spirit so that it might one day be reborn, reopened to God's presence, and God's presence alone.

Left adrift without guidance of a spirit, what were Adam and Eve to do? They succumbed to control, the very nature of satan, who had manipulated, dominated, and intimidated Adam and Eve into selling their souls! With God shut out of the spirit and the devil invited into the soul, control became the human *modus operandi*.

Two or Three Parts to the Whole?

The difference between Hebraic and Greek understandings of human ontology interestingly portrays the reality that humans, since the Fall and apart from *life* in Christ Jesus, are bipartite beings, operating only in body and soul.

As shared before, the Greek word for "soul" is *psuche*. The Hebrew word is *nephesh*, but the real difference comes in terms of definition. As Donald McKim has pointed out, "For Hebrews, it indicated the unity of the person as a living body."[3] In Hebraic thought, concepts like oneness, unity, and wholeness in terms of God and humanity are predominant. In Greek thought, the focus is more on the uniqueness of the parts that make up the whole. Greek thought helps us identify the "threeness" of God, while Hebraic thought reminds us that *"The Lord our God…is one!"* (Deut. 6:4).

In terms of the Fall, with the spirit closed and the soul and body hopelessly intertwined in brokenness, the Hebraic concept was both accurate and, for all practical purposes, complete. Furthermore, it reminds us of the limits God placed on Himself when He lovingly closed our spirits to save our lives and eventually reestablish full triune relationship. The biblical term *flesh (sarx)* helps confirm this. While the literal meaning of the word describes the physical body, common usage of the word combines the soul and body in describing the sinful seat of our fallen desires. Hence, Jesus could say to His sleepy disciples at Gethsemane, *"Watch and pray, lest you enter into temptation. The spirit indeed is willing, but the flesh is weak"* (Matt. 26:41).

With the spirit sealed off, the only way of appeal left for God was through the physical nature, the body, with the hope that the person would open his or her soul to God's advances. The Old Testament is an amazing picture of rituals, feasts, laws, and worship designed to open one's life to the Person of God. God approached through the only way left possible, the realm of physical sense: sight, sound, smell, and taste. It is through these physical senses that one's conscience (the soulish realm) is awakened to the reality of God, a reality no one can deny (see Rom. 1). Simultaneously, the First Covenant is also a giant, panoramic, and prophetic picture of God's ultimate plan. Unable to breathe Spirit to spirit, God devised the ultimate plan of coming as a human being, thus allowing His own people (and ultimately all people) to see, experience, and enjoy His presence.[4]

With Jesus, God the Son, present, the Hebraic concept had to be supplemented, but never replaced, with a deeper understanding of the Triune reality of God, as well as the triune reality of humanity. Luke 2:40 reminds us that young Jesus became *"strong in spirit,"* while Luke 2:52 reminds us that He grew in *"wisdom* [soul] *and stature* [body]. *"* Jesus came as a fully Tripartite Human, the first since Adam and Eve, so that people could once again experience God, Face-to-face. However, He came to do more: He came to redeem (buy back) humanity with the goal of reopening the spirit of the redeemed and restoring the triune relationship with God. With spirit reborn and the fullness of God breathing *within* again, disciples become fully tripartite beings with the spirit once again alive and breathing, the soul under repair, and a new body on the way.

Of Full Salvation and Entire Sanctification

It should be clear that Adam and Eve enjoyed full relationship with the fullness of God. Father, Son, and Holy Spirit—One God—communed with them in wholeness. When our spirit is reborn, it is God's intent that all He is will be received. He invites us to allow Him to immerse us in repentance, into an intimate friendship with Jesus, and with the power and Person of the Holy Spirit, all these Three as One. Paul has said we are saved by grace through faith as a gift (see Eph. 2:8), not by works, effort, religion, sweat, or tears. It is all a gift! But what is "it"? "It" is grace, the power of God. "It" is *full salvation*, everything salvation encompasses, and *entire sanctification*, everything that holiness entails. God wants to impart to us a fullness of grace, all of it a gift, that completely fills and restores our human spirit to its original perfection. Once accomplished, our spirit can then "set the course" for the restoration of our soul in preparation for our new body.

John Wesley expounded the belief that our spirit should be, not only alive, but also *full* by the grace of God in the life of a Christian. He irritated more than a few of his contemporaries (most of whom were stuck in bipartite thinking) with the notion that Christians could and should be entirely and completely set apart, assured of their election, and empowered with the Holy Spirit. He did not confuse the spirit with the soul. He did not confuse the instantaneous reception of grace in the spirit with the process of maturity (perfection) in the soul. He did not confuse God's *grace* with Christian *growth*. The one is received, by faith, in fullness; the other is a process of becoming *in the soul* what God has already accomplished *in the spirit*. Wesley believed that we should receive the fullness of God entirely (because it is a free gift, grace!), and then, with God's love and acceptance anchoring our spirit, progress to the only logical point: perfection in the soul.

We need to understand Wesley's concept. In the opening moments of our walk with God, we can and should seek and desire a full impartation of grace in our spirit. With this fullness in the spirit in place, the fullness that Christian baptism so powerfully portrays, the working out of our salvation (and sanctification) can take place in our soul. We really grow up because we are really in the "grip of grace."

But what happens when the spirit is reborn, but not full? What happens when justification is received, but sanctification is not? With a dwarfed reception of grace in the spirit, a person is destined to a dwarfed maturing process in the soul. Wesley realized how badly we need all the grace God offers, and as soon as possible, in order for true maturity to take place. Thus, based on First Thessalonians 5:23, Wesley encouraged "entire sanctification" to believers *as they begin their walk,* trusting in the fact that grace is a gift and that, once the gift is in place, the "work" of maturity can begin in earnest. Once the assurance of salvation is in place, and once believers, by the Holy Spirit, choose to love God with all of their heart, soul, and strength (spirit, soul, and body!), the lifelong process of growth and maturity (*"perfection"* in Hebrews 6:1) can safely progress to God's desired outcome *in this life.*

Control and Cheap Grace

Since control is rooted in the human soul (a sick gift from satan), it is the maturing process that must root it out. As Wesley would argue, this process can never fully happen unless and until a person has received the fullness of grace which is the gift of the Father, Son, and Holy Spirit, grace which is a full expression of Him *in the human spirit.* We need to be fully saved and completely set apart in order for the grace imparted to fully impact our mind, will, and emotions.

Bonhoeffer coined the term "Cheap grace." He described it, in part, as:

> The preaching of forgiveness without requiring repentance, baptism without church discipline, Communion without

confession, absolution without personal confession. Cheap grace is grace without discipleship, grace without the cross, grace without Jesus Christ, living and incarnate.[5]

Cheap grace is the great travesty of the modern American Church. Salvation is often presented in terms of mouthing a short forgiveness prayer with no hint of repentance. Other times it is presented as a universal gift to all who endure church services, or take a membership pledge, or are just breathing. We have so cheapened *new birth* that millions of churchgoers are still living under *old death*, although they are oblivious to the fact!

Far too many Christians have reduced the concept of an intimate relationship with Jesus to "going to Heaven someday." Still others have reduced the baptism with the Holy Spirit to a vague sense of entitlement (you get Him when you are baptized with water). Perhaps even worse, some equate baptism with the Holy Spirit with a mandatory public display of speaking in tongues (oftentimes only once—"requirement" met, job finished!). What a travesty!

Real grace involves real repentance, a powerful turning around accomplished only by grace. Real grace involves a genuine, ongoing, life-giving, vibrant relationship with God the Son. Real grace involves the Spirit flowing through our heart (spirit) like a river (see John 7) with gifts, power, and transformation so real *and ongoing* as to make us true witnesses (see Acts 1).

In Wesleyan language, *prevenient grace* (the grace that goes before and woos one to God) always has as its target *repentance*. God doesn't just woo us to make us feel warm and fuzzy; His "going before" grace is given to bring us to a specific goal: genuine repentance.

Justifying grace also has a goal, *a deeply real and intimate relationship with Jesus.* Often this grace is presented so cheaply, as a vague sense of belonging to the church or "going to Heaven" someday, rather than an ongoing relationship with the Justifier. Justification is so much more than a declaration of "not guilty"! Walking out of prison is nice; walking arm in arm with the One who paid for the release is far better!

Sanctifying grace has as its goal the complete immersion of the person (starting with the spirit) into the life-transforming, gift-giving, fruit-bearing flow of the *Holy Spirit*. Again, it is often (cheaply) presented in terms of "growing up" (as if that's possible without the Spirit)! Self-effort and hard work are not synonymous with Christian maturity. Avoiding movies, makeup, and making-out may certainly provide some benefits to a practitioner, but they do not, in themselves, constitute sanctification!

The result of all this cheap grace is a severe spirit-anemia in many churchgoing people that precludes any real hope of soul-change. Control stays firmly rooted because real *grace* has not been received. Maturity never happens because the believer's spirit is never strong enough to take leadership over the soul.

The Spirit-House Must Be Full

There is a difference between the Holy Spirit "within us" (see Ezek. 11:19) and the Holy Spirit "upon us" (see Joel 2:28). There is a difference between a *"fountain of water springing up into everlasting life"* (John 4:14) and *"rivers of living water"* flowing out of the human heart (John 7:38). There is a difference between Jesus' breathing on disciples (see John 20:22) and His baptizing them with the Holy Spirit (see Acts 1:5). There is a difference—a tremendous difference— between the human spirit being reopened and the human spirit being filled and fully restored.

At great cost to the individual as well as the Church, some of our theological "boxes" fail to make the distinctions mentioned above. Far too many churchgoing, Jesus-loving folks have been taught a truncated faith that stops with initial salvation, denying the necessity of Spirit-fullness. Yet Matthew 12:43-45 warns of the costliness of a house *"swept"* and *"put in order,"* but still *"empty."* As well as picturing the danger of Israel's empty religiousness of Jesus' day, these verses graphically describe the dangers of empty religiousness in every age. God did not intend for people to simply be born again of "water" (true repentance, with or without physical water), but also to be born of the Holy Spirit (see John 3:5). New birth must occur: Jesus must breathe life back into the spirit; however, new birth is just the beginning, not the finish.

Taken seriously, Matthew 12:43-45 indicates the chilling reality that a house just "swept" and "in order" poses the danger of demonic "filling." The reference clearly portends the fact of an "empty house" attracting demons. Judging by church history, one would have to assume that it is religious demons that are especially attracted to those empty places. Much of the religiosity and control-ism seen (and often accepted as normal!) in the Church is a direct result of clean-but-Holy-Spirit-deprived houses. Religious demons, after all, get a thrill over all the angry emotions, gossip, intrigue, division and outright hatred generated in, of all places, the Church!

The key, then, is to seek and submit to God's full package, the "Promise of the Father" (see Luke 24:49). When our human spirit is full with all of God, there is no room for the demonic, and there is tremendous assurance that we can indeed experience life-changing transformation in our flesh (soul and body).

In Summary

Satan approached Adam and Eve in the realm of the soul, convincing them that they could "be like God." The devil knew what he was doing, based on his own fall, and based on his wielding of control (domination, manipulation, intimidation) to grotesquely mimic the perfect reigning of God. Human souls have believed the lie ever since. Apart from the human spirit alive with God's fullness, the soul will attempt to control people, places, and things in a grotesque mimicking of God's perfect rule and reign.

Our soul, therefore, *must* be healed, transformed from glory to glory as we behold the Lord (see 2 Cor. 3:14-18). However, before we can be transformed from one level of glory to the next and eventually look like Jesus, the "veil" must be taken away by Christ. Salvation is the starting point. Before our soul can be transformed—certainly before it can be transformed to the point of reflecting the image of

Jesus rather than satan's—our spirit must be filled with all the fullness of God.

Our *spirit* was designed to be full of God's presence, not just open to it, so that our *soul* can see Jesus by the Holy Spirit and take on His image. The work of restoring the soul is a progressive work of transformation. Both the rebirth and the filling of the human spirit are absolutely and totally grace. They come instantly if we are open, not only to Jesus' breathing upon us the Holy Spirit, but also to His baptizing us with the Holy Spirit. They are ours if we are open to both justification and sanctification, if we are open to both a *"fountain of water"* (John 4:14) and *"rivers of living water"* (John 8:38).

Sadly, too many have not opened themselves to the both-and of God's grace. Too many human spirits are "swept" but empty; too many, still trapped in playing God; too many, still trying to be in control. Like the Sadducees of Jesus' day, many Christians today are mistaken, *"not knowing the Scriptures nor the power of God"* (Matt. 22:29).

In view of having all that God intends for us, we need to ask ourselves three questions:

1. Is my spirit full of all the grace that's available? Am I, in baptismal language, "wet" with repentance of the Father, intimacy in the Son, and the power of the Holy Spirit? If not, I need to ask and seek the fullness of God's promise!

2. Is my soul being transformed daily into the Lord's image? Am I being *"conformed to this world"* or *"transformed by the renewing of* [my] *mind* [and will and emotion]"? If not, I need to present myself to God *"as a living sacrifice"* (Romans 12:1-2).

3. Is my spirit in charge of my life, or is my soul (and body)? Do my thoughts and lusts and feelings set the course for my life, or does the reign and breath of God over and *in* me set the course? If soul and body have too much sway (too often they do for all of us!), I need to discover the power of praying in the Holy Spirit, the power of daily time in the Word and the power of a daily cross to set my triune nature in proper order!

Plug-ins, Power, and Completed Circuits

We need to picture ourselves as electrical cords. We are created to perfectly plug in to the *Source*, our Creator—the outlet. Plugged in, we have life; unplugged, we are dead! The full extent of the Creator's purposes for the cord can be seen only when the power is flowing and the circuit is complete, when the cord is both connected to the outlet and full of current, purpose, and flow. Our spirit is the *plug-in*, our soul, the *wire;* our body, the *insulation* containing the wire and plug. We are dead until God's grace plugs us in again. We become useful as God's grace fills us and flows through us to accomplish His purposes. We again experience the life for which we were created as His *current* (repentance, intimacy, and power) flows to and through us—spirit, soul, and body.

Chapter Five

CONTROL IS MURDER!

I'll make a dangerous confession for a preacher: Until not long ago, the whole Cain/Abel story didn't quite make sense to me. Perhaps, like me, you get excited over the prospect that those passages, stories, and concepts in Scripture that you don't presently comprehend fully will one day come alive to you by the Spirit. I sure do. Well, the Cain and Abel story came alive for me not long ago, and it has become a powerful picture for me.

I figured out early on in my faith walk that when I don't understand something in the Bible, the problem isn't with the Scripture. The Word of God is completely reliable and God-breathed. There are just things I'm not mature enough or ready to comprehend yet. And because the Scripture is living and breathing and multilayered, there are enough levels and concepts and applications to last an eternity. So I've learned to just wait (fairly) patiently for the Lord to make revelation available when I read something and it doesn't quite "click" for me. Well that happened with the fourth chapter of Genesis (I waited and God made it click!) and I'd like to share that with you now.

Genesis 4:1-8 states:

> *Now Adam knew Eve his wife, and she conceived and bore Cain, and said, "I have acquired a man from the Lord." Then she bore again, this time his brother Abel. Now Abel was a*

keeper of sheep, but Cain was a tiller of the ground. And in the process of time it came to pass that Cain brought an offering of the fruit of the ground to the Lord. Abel also brought of the firstborn of his flock and of their fat. And the Lord respected Abel and his offering, but He did not respect Cain and his offering. And Cain was very angry, and his countenance fell. So the Lord said to Cain, "Why are you angry? And why has your countenance fallen? If you do well, will you not be accepted? And if you do not do well, sin lies at the door. And its desire is for you, but you should rule over it." Now Cain talked with Abel his brother; and it came to pass, when they were in the field, that Cain rose up against Abel his brother and killed him.

Both Cain and Abel had the same background. Both had seen the tunics of skin their parents wore. Surely they had heard the story about the fig leaves, portraying the kind of sacrifice God desires—one that resembles and reflects the grace of the tunic, not the self-effort of the fig leaves. Works have never been an acceptable offering to God! He doesn't want our *religion!* He wants a relationship based on our being clothed in an innocent Substitute! The Lord does not desire offerings that come about through our control, our manipulating, dominating, or intimidating. He wants offerings that come through His dressing us, through His shed blood, in His nature. Abel's offering was a reflection of the blood that would be shed for the free gift of salvation; Cain's, an offering of produce that looked remarkably like fig leaves. Cain attempted to please God by doing things his own way instead of following the pattern typified by the tunics his parents wore. His offering was a reflection of man's works, man's own efforts to manipulate, dominate, and intimidate his relationship with God. Without this understanding, the story of Cain and Abel makes no sense. Without this understanding, Cain, whose offering was unacceptable to God, may become the sympathetic character instead of Abel, whose offering pleased God. In his offering, Cain manifested satan's character; Abel, the Lord's!

As the story continues, we see Cain given an opportunity to repent and offer an acceptable sacrifice, something that would glory in God's work, not his own. God always offers a way of escape, a way out of our fallen, controlling, "you-can-be-like-God" nature. However, true to the ontology of satan acquired in the Fall, Cain went out and murdered Abel. In Cain's murderous *attitude* we see religion in its most basic form: fallen attitudes lead to fallen actions. In Cain's murderous action, we see control in all its raw ugliness, control carried to its ultimate degree. Ultimately, controlling others is about *murdering* their preferences on one's own altar. Dominating, manipulating, and intimidating are all fruit from the farm of self-rule and self-effort. Offered to God, they do not please Him; they look like fig leaves, not tunics.

The New Testament reminds us that all who believe are priests. Like Cain and Abel, we must bring sacrifices before the Lord. The New Testament names three sacrifices to be offered to the Lord: the sacrifice of *praise* (see Heb. 13:15), the sacrifice of *sharing* (see Heb. 13:16), and the sacrifice of *self* (see Rom. 12:1). In each case, the sacrifice resembles and reflects the glory of Jesus. All picture doing God's things God's way. They are about God's effort on our behalf, not about our own efforts. When we spend our lives dying to self, sharing with others, and praising God rather than trying to manipulate, intimidate, or dominate others, we are offering to God an Abel sort of sacrifice, one that is pleasing and acceptable to God. Although control may afford pleasure in the flesh and build up a "big farm," this fruit is rotten before God. Instead of murdering the Abel in others, we must die to the Cain within!

We Resemble What We Worship

A parallel concept to the whole Cain and Abel picture is the fact that we humans begin to resemble the very thing we worship. If we worship God, we ever more fully resemble Him. If we worship control, even for the sake of being a strong leader in the church, we resemble, ever more fully, satan in all of his fallen nature.

As we look at the Israelites in the wilderness, we see a salient example of becoming what we worship. The generation God delivered from Egypt had the opportunity to look like God in His righteousness, in all of His promise. They could have experienced His presence in dramatic ways. They could have looked remarkably like God; yet they spent the rest of their lives wandering around like cattle, having chosen to build and worship a golden calf while Moses was on the mountain of God's presence. Having chosen to worship the creation of their own hands rather than the glory of God's hands, they forfeited the opportunity of resting in God's promise in His promised land. They became like the very thing they worshiped!

When we worship the "power" that control gives us, the golden calf of manipulation, intimidation, or domination, we begin to resemble control more and more and the God of our deliverance less and less. Tragically, we see this same pattern in many of today's Church leaders, *Aarons* who build golden calves. Some of them develop enormously successful ministries empowered not by the grace of God but by the work of human hands. These churches and ministries fail, however, because they ultimately resemble the very thing they worship, be it "prosperity" or "relevance" or whatever, rather than the Lord Himself. People flock to an "Aaron." People *want* an "Aaron"; however, we all *need* a "Moses." Church people *want* chaplains, but we *need* shepherds. We need leaders who insist we worship nothing but the Lord, recognizing that we will ultimately resemble what we worship. Too often we get chaplains who just want to keep the "herd" happy. The result is an awful lot of "cattle" wandering around directionless, clueless, stiff-necked, and rebellious, "mooing" in complaint constantly, but never arriving at the goal.

A glaring and disastrous contemporary example of *calf-building* comes from my own tradition. We United Methodists, like other mainliners, have decided to build a golden calf called "inclusive language." The goal not to use language that excludes people, particularly because of gender, seemed laudable enough. Thus, "mankind" became "humankind;" "manhood" became "personhood." So far, so good! Marginalization and discrimination against women has been one of the most regrettable scandals of the whole Church Age, and sexism, of course, is control. However, the effort to avoid *sexist* language became an attack on the self-revelation of God. It became taboo to refer to God as "He,"or even to Christ as "Jesus." Thus, we sing songs like *"God's got the whole world in God's hands."*

Not only does inclusive language result in changes that are awkward and silly; it also strikes at the very heart of relationship. Clearly, it flows from the demonic seat of control. When personal pronouns, God-chosen ones at that, are forbidden and replaced with impersonal and distant titles, relationship suffers until only religion is left. How can anyone be close to an *It*? Or to a "God self" instead of a "Father"? Or to a Jesus who is an anomaly, neither male nor female? What happens to what we have cherished so much, a relationship with Father, Son, and Holy Spirit? Despite what may have been an admirable objective, the exclusions of inclusive language have morphed into a religion of controlling people—intimidating, manipulating, and dominating—through language! Thus, we wander around like politically-correct cattle, proud and stiff-necked in our language, but dead to the intimate, first-name-basis relationship God offers and desires.

The question we must ask ourselves is this: Are we worshiping the Lord in all of His dominion and authority and glory, or are we worshiping control through intimidation, manipulation, and domination, and the short-lived, fallen, demonic power it brings? We must never forget that satan has always dressed up control, the power of his fallen nature, into things that seem "like God." We must be careful lest we fall for his lies and worship him, thus becoming more like him than like God.

How Baptized Are We?

Acts 18 gives us an amazing insight into one of God's primary weapons in combating the control nature within us humans. We find Apollos preaching with eloquence and fervency. Still, to Aquila and Priscilla (and the Lord!), there was something obviously missing in Apollos. While Apollos *"taught accurately the things of the Lord...he knew only the baptism of John"* (Acts 18:25). The text goes on to say that Aquila and Priscilla *"took him aside and explained to him the way of God more accurately"* (Acts 18:26).

It is obvious that Apollos was baptized, but not *fully* baptized. He was "wet" with repentance (the baptism of John), but not wet in all the ways God desires us to be wet. If we are going to operate in the "way of God more accurately," then we must understand what full Christian baptism is, and be dripping wet in it (Him!).

Not surprisingly, Christian baptism is triune in nature. We are to be baptized *by* the Father, *into* Christ Jesus, and *with* the Holy Spirit. God desires that we be wet with *all* of Him. But, like Apollos, many of us, bound by our traditions and their limits of accuracy, are ignorant to the fullness baptism is intended to be. Nothing will dislodge our control nature (the core of our being which looks like and seeks power like satan) like a good and ongoing soaking in Father, Son, and Holy Spirit!

First, Christian baptism is an immersion, *initial and ongoing*, in *repentance*, the "baptism of John." It is in particular the gift of the Father, whose "kindness leads us to repentance" (see Rom. 2:4). In order to be in relationship with the Father, there must be *our* desire and *His* power to "turn around" (repent) and go His way. When we "drip" with initial and ongoing repentance, we are equipped to lay down the controlling nature within us that desires to go our own way rather then turn around and go God's way.

Satan never repented. His character and nature are disgusting reminders of that fact, and a heartrending picture of what our *ontology* looks like without the immersion of repentance!

Second, Christian baptism is an immersion, *initial and ongoing*, *into Jesus*. *"For as many of you as were baptized into Christ have put on Christ"* (Gal. 3:27). This baptism of *intimacy* soaks us in the Person of Jesus, His death and resurrection (see Romans 6:3-14), and into the unity of His Body (see Gal. 3:26-28). In short, being baptized into Christ immerses believers into *everything* Jesus came, died, and rose again to give us. In order to be in relationship with Jesus, we must be dripping wet with His nature and essence! Talk about a powerful way to counteract the fallen nature we were born with!

Satan fled from intimacy from God, and our human nature desires to flee as well. Remember when the Israelites fled from the presence of

God at Mount Sinai? (See Exodus 20:18-21.) They were simply acting out of their (and our) basic nature. But when we are immersed into Christ Jesus, we begin to drip with a life-changing intimacy with God that defines our new, born-again nature. Instead of running *away from* His presence, we begin to desire to run *toward* His presence. Our natural inclination to control begins to give way to Jesus' reign and rule in and through us as we soak in intimacy with Him.

Third, Christian baptism is an immersion, *initial and ongoing*, with the power and presence of the Holy Spirit. As Acts 1:8 says, *"But you shall receive power when the Holy Spirit has come upon you; and you shall be witnesses to Me in Jerusalem, and in all Judea and Samaria, and to the end of the earth."* This "Promise of the Father" (Acts 1:4) is for all who are baptized in Christ Jesus and in the repentance of the Father. But without this immersion with the Holy Spirit, we are crippled in witness and in power. Signs and wonders, Spirit-gifted language, prophecy, healings, and building-shaking prayer and praise—these were the norms of the early Church. Why? Because when disciples like Apollos (or the 12 mentioned in Acts 19), were discovered by fully-baptized believers, they were prayed with and instructed immediately.

Apollos and the Ephesian disciples were *baptized*, but not *fully baptized*. They were disciples but not yet witnesses; so Paul and Aquila and Priscilla did the only loving thing they could do. They led these partially-baptized disciples into full Christian baptism—*repentance* of the Father, *intimacy* in the Son, and *power* from the Holy Spirit!

Satan never submitted to the power of the Holy Spirit, choosing to operate in his own instead. This power is what we have been calling *control*, and until we are washed in the waters of full Christian baptism, it is the only power we know. We are born "baptized" into satan's character and nature, and we are bound to it (him!) until we are baptized in repentance, intimacy, and power, into the fullness of all of the Triune God.

Acts 2:38 is a great summary verse describing full Christian baptism:

> *Then Peter said to them, "Repent, and let every one of you be baptized in the name of Jesus Christ for the remission of sins; and you shall receive the gift of the Holy Spirit.*

Repent—immersed in Jesus, receiving the Holy Spirit. No wonder the 3,000 baptized on the Day of Pentecost were so wet with God! The problem is that we modern Christians tend to cram all this wetness into small theological boxes, resulting in far too many dry disciples!

Is infant baptism the culprit? Is an insistence on water immersion the problem? Is an emphasis on repentance while ignoring power the problem? Is an emphasis on membership in a church rather than intimacy with Jesus the problem? "Yes" to all these and many more! How we American Christians, by and large, could have messed up baptism so badly is almost a mystery. We get so hung up over the depth and temperature of the water, style, language, age of the participant, etc., that we seem, almost universally, to miss the crux of the matter—*being wet with all of God and staying under the fountain!*

Some would argue that simply being baptized in repentance means that one is "saved," and that is good enough. Some would argue that baptism is a "package deal," and we get all of it in the dunking. Some would argue that baptism is a once-in-a-lifetime experience that dare not be repeated. Argue those points with Paul! Argue them with Peter and John! (See Acts 8:14-17.) Argue them with Aquila and Priscilla! Ask Apollos or the disciples in Ephesus if they regretted getting more baptized (note that *water was optional*, but not the full wetness of God)!

While it may be true that everyone being baptized in our various churches *should* be fully wet in repentance, intimacy, and power, fully wet *of* the Father, *in* the Son, and *with* the Holy Spirit, the obvious truth is that many (in fact, most!) are not. And many of us are drying out with far too few baptismal experiences along the way to stay wet! Our theological boxes are too shallow. Our concept of baptism is too narrow. Our reduction of the Gospel to "being saved" and "going to Heaven" is way too small. We worship the water or the tank or the liturgy and forget about the Triune relationship the water, baptistery, and liturgy merely *represent*.

Beware of Dry Places...

Why were Peter and John and Paul and Aquila and Priscilla so insistent when dealing with folks like Apollos who were only partially baptized? Clearly, these early disciples knew that, without being fully baptized, Apollos was in grave danger of demonic invasion. No doubt they remembered Jesus' very words of warning, recorded in Matthew 12:43-45:

> *When an unclean spirit goes out of a man, he goes through dry places, seeking rest, and finds none. Then he says, "I will return to my house from which I came." And when he comes, he finds it empty, swept, and put in order. Then he goes and takes with him seven other spirits more wicked than himself, and they enter and dwell there; and the last state of that man is worse than the first. So shall it be with this wicked generation.*

Jesus' words show that dry places attract the demonic realm. A house/life swept clean and put in order draws demons because it is empty. The only house/life safe from demonic invasion is one that is full and wet with the presence of the Lord. Although partial baptism may *cleanse*, it does not *fill*. Being repulsively wet and full of the fullness of the Godhead is the only defense against the unclean spirits seeking dry places to invade!

Actually, Apollos and the others were in danger of being drawn back to legalism, or drawn away into heresy, or rendered impotent by constant attack. What they didn't know, and what they hadn't experienced, had the potential of destroying them. Thus, the early Church acted swiftly and definitively to see that Apollos and the others received full Christian baptism. Oh that today's disciples would operate in that kind of boldness and discernment! If the Church today were as responsible as the Church of the first century in making sure that all believers were fully and continually wet with God, many lives would be spared and empowered and used of the Lord.

When a believer is fully baptized of/in/with the Father, Son, and Holy Spirit, wet with repentance, intimacy, and power, then our "original baptism" by satan with domination, intimidation, and manipulation is progressively washed away. The dryness of *control* gives way to the wetness of holiness. However, as long as we remain only partially baptized, we remain particularly vulnerable to the fallen nature we were born with, and to demonic realities that are drawn to it.

Full Christian baptism combats our fallen control nature with supernatural efficiency and effectiveness! Being wet with God helps to ensure that we worship *Him*, not various golden calves. Being wet with God helps to ensure that we offer sacrifices which look like God's grace, not our self-efforts. Being wet with God discourages demonic attack. Being wet with God breaks the murderous power of the control nature. Our primary concern should be about how wet we are as a congregation and as individuals.

...But Not of Dry Cleaning!

To be sure, we must always guard against dry places, the un-baptized or under-baptized areas in our lives. However, we should also encourage lots of "dry cleaning"!

Because we (at least in my part of the country) have built such a monument to water (and lots of it), we forget that Apollos' "more accurate" baptism occurred without water. Properly understood, baptism for a Christian is not optional, but water is optional. The repentant thief on the cross was baptized—immersed—without a hint of sprinkling, pouring, or dunking. His repentance itself was a baptism, as was his request to be in intimate relationship with the Lord.

We forget that baptism has a whole lot to do with God, but very little to do with us. More problematic is the reality that many folks in our pews have been sold a bill of goods of sorts. Although they may have been soaking wet with water baptism, they are absolutely dry in relationship with God. We have built the false altar of the baptistery and the golden calf of membership numbers, replacing relationship with God for a moment's tingle in water and a name in *our* book.

One of the powerful aspects of (water) baptism is the sense that it is a defining moment in a believer's life. On the other hand, repentance, intimacy, and empowerment cannot be once-in-a-lifetime experiences; we humans dry out too fast! Obviously, these three aspects of relationship with the Triune God must be the ongoing fabric of our church life. Since the symbol (water) should remain something of a memorial stone, there must be "Apollos" moments built into our daily and weekly walk as Christians to make sure that we are being baptized and baptized and baptized some more, via "dry cleaning."

We need to allow and encourage many, many "defining moments" without wearing out the water spigot. As we make room for ongoing repentance, ever-deepening intimacy, and being filled and filled and filled (see. Eph 5:18) with the Spirit, we need to highlight and celebrate these baptismal cleansings and restorations as defining moments, truly baptisms, not just "goose bump" events. Real encounters with the fullness of the Godhead deserve recognition and celebration!

There is a difference between a prayer of repentance and a *baptism* of repentance. There is a difference between a moment of intimacy with Jesus and a new level, a *baptism into Christ*. There is a difference between an initial "Pentecost" and ongoing Pentecostal baptisms. We need to think in terms of "Ebenezers" (life-changing events), not just quickly forgotten experiences.

A Baptized Theology

A brief review of what was said in Chapter Four might help here. We humans were created as tripartite beings: spirit, soul, and body. The Fall required God to shut off our spirit (to protect us and allow a way of redemption), thus allowing our soul to lead—right into satan's character. Pre-Jesus, we function as bipartite beings: soul and body. At the revelational moment when we know Jesus as *"the Christ, the Son of the living God"* (Matt. 16:16), our spirit is born again. In original righteousness, our spirit, in perfect union with the Holy Spirit, set the course for our soul and body. As Adam and Eve "danced" perfectly within themselves, they also danced perfectly with each other and with God. Too soon, however, the *dance* ended.

In order for our human spirit once again to set the course for our soul and body, it must not only be reborn; it must also be filled. This is the initial "wetness" I've described. Our spirit needs to be immersed in repentance, immersed in intimate friendship with Jesus, and immersed in the fullness of the Holy Spirit. The good and great news is that all is by grace, not by our efforts. We don't deserve or earn full salvation and entire sanctification; they are gifts. Father, Son, and Holy Spirit want the house of our spirit to be full, not just clean!

The early Church was keenly aware of this need for fullness. *In every single instance* where a disciple was found who lacked one or another aspect of full Christian baptism, the Church responded definitively. The eighth chapter of Acts depicts this pattern. Upon hearing that *"Samaria had received the word of God"* (Acts 8:14), the apostles in Jerusalem sent Peter and John to them. Upon their arrival, Peter and John discerned that, although the people had been baptized in water (in the baptism of intimacy), they were yet dry. Consequently, *"they laid hands on them, and they received the Holy Spirit"* (Acts 8:17). Next, they dealt with Simon the Sorcerer, who obviously needed a baptism of repentance. In Acts 10 (at Cornelius' house), we see Peter and company immersing in waters of repentance and intimacy the gentile converts who had (moments before) experienced baptism with the Holy Spirit. In Acts 18:26, we read about Aquila and Priscilla taking Apollos aside, explaining *"to him the way of God more accurately"* because he knew *"only the baptism of John."* Then, in Acts 19:1-7, we see Paul water baptizing about a dozen men *into* Jesus and *hands* baptizing them with the Holy Spirit. Previously, these 12 had known only the baptism of John (repentance). Paul immersed them, with water and with hands, into full Christian baptism: repentance, intimacy, and power.

Once a human *spirit* is fully baptized, it is *fully baptized*! We cannot get more of God than all of Him! The question then becomes whether or not He has all of us in our *soul*. It is in the realm of the soul where *ongoing wetness* is needed. *Ongoing,* of course, indicates an initial experience of being fully *wet*. Simply stated, we need a complete Christian baptism in our spirit, and ongoing baptisms in our soul. In one sense, baptism is once-for-all; in the other, a never-ending need until and unless our soul is perfected.

Since the spirit should once again set the course for a believer's life, it is absolutely imperative that it be completely full and wet. Without full baptism in our spirit, it is impossible for our soul to ever truly reach maturity. A huge source of the religiosity and churchianity and controlism in our midst is the reality of partially baptized church members who still control by the soul, thereby being incapable of true maturity.

By grace, we should seek and submit ourselves—our spirit being—to full baptism. *By grace*, we should enjoy the fruit of full baptism as our soul submits to washing after washing, immersion after immersion. The goal? For our soul to grow up and look like the fullness of God already deposited in our spirit!

The Cross: The Only Way to the Baptistery

In the Tabernacle of old and the Temple that followed, one had to pass by the altar of sacrifice before they came to the bronze laver of water. In most church sanctuaries, the cross is the central feature, with the baptistery behind or to the side of it. The picture is clear: one must deal with the cross before entering the baptistery. The cross is the altar of the New Testament, and the only way to the baptistery is through the sacrifice of the cross. The human soul requires repeated (daily!) death in order to be washed in the grace of repeated baptisms. We need to be wet with God, all of Him, all the time. But His "wetness" is a gift for those who have first paused and sacrificed themselves at the cost of dead flesh on the altar of sacrifice, the cross. Baptism begins with the sacrifice of Jesus on the cross, and continues only as the sacrifice of a daily cross leads one to the baptistery. Dying to self and rising to new life wet in Jesus is the rhythm of true Christian relationship, and relationship is the heart of Christian baptism.

We really must get this straight: Father, Son, and Holy Spirit want a *relationship* with us, not ritual-keeping. *Baptism is essentially relational* as God reignites full relationship in our spirit and begins the process of releasing the grace to transform our souls. Eventually, He'll give us a new body, because He wants all of us, spirit, soul, and body, to know—to be immersed in—all of Him!

Chapter Six

THE GAME OF CONTROL

In the opening pages of this book, I shared about my "war" with the church treasurer and the painful but revelation-filled trip that followed. In short, I (the pastor) lied to the treasurer one day in early 2000, attempting to manipulate myself out of a sticky situation with a person I loved but who repeatedly intimidated me as well as others in my congregation. As I drove to Muncie, Indiana, I reflected on the unpleasant encounter I'd had. Thinking about my use of manipulation and the treasurer's use of intimidation brought to mind other church leaders who try to reign by domination.

The Lord then clearly spoke three words to me: *domination, intimidation,* and *manipulation.* At the same time, He gave me a picture of the game Rock/Paper/Scissors. Immediately, I saw a connection between *Rock* and *Domination; Paper* and *Manipulation;* and *Scissors* and *Intimidation.* The core of the book was developing in my mind!

I recognized that no one wins in this *game* because no one method is better than another; what works in one situation fails in the next. Besides, the whole *game* is fundamentally wrong. By revelation of God, I saw that the game of control, using the means of the three words He spoke to me, is satan's way of ruling in this present age. Furthermore, we humans, by the Fall, are born in and under this wretched nature of control!

As I continued to reflect upon the analogy God had given me, I realized that all of us are born playing this game, despite the fact that it is a stupid game on which to base one's life. Even more disconcerting was the realization that all of us are doomed, without divine intervention, to keep playing this fallen, wicked game that flows from satan's warped heart. I saw that, ultimately, this game is no game at all. It is the destructive reality of living life in the vacuum of satan's fallen character. In tears, I repented of playing the game with my treasurer. Ever since I have been trying to lead others to die to their control nature.

As I shared earlier, I have discovered that there is an amazing lack of good teaching in this area. In fact, I have seen repeatedly an oblivious inability to recognize that control is the antithesis of God's character. Thus, in church after church, we appoint, promote, and glory in control freaks who may be saved, but who, both pastors and laity, wield the rock/paper/scissors of control rather than the sword of the Spirit. Yes, there are congregations where the presence of the Lord is so cherished that the control nature is diminished, whether or not anyone in the congregation has taken the time to define, expose, or reject it. However, such a congregation is far too rare!

So How Did Control Become Our Problem?

The question then arises: How did control become our problem? The answer lies in the fact that an ontological transfer occurred in The Garden. We bought satan's lie that we would be "like God." We exchanged domination for control. Like Adam and Eve, we are dressed in the fig leaves of self-effort and shame. We exchanged a naked intimacy for a leafy disguise. Having given the title deed to "father" satan, we have resorted to trying to fix the mess by satan's method of control. Trying to fix what's broken by the very nature of brokenness is insane; yet that insanity—apart from Christ—is the human condition.

Control in all forms, of course, is sin. Domination is just as demonic as intimidation, which is just as demonic as manipulation. There is no preferred method of behaving like the devil! And let it be remembered that control is completely natural to us. We are born with the fallen precept that this is the way to live on earth. Born with the innate tendency to control, we honestly think, deep inside ourselves, that we can make the world a better place through control. We read self-help books and, perhaps, even attend seminars to learn how to be more "successful" manipulators or dominators or intimidators. Thus, we lead our businesses and churches by "playing" Rock/Paper/Scissors, winning some and losing some, but hurting everyone including ourselves along the way. And more often than not, we are often absolutely oblivious to what we are doing.

Perhaps it would help to define the three components of the control nature:

> **Domination:** To dominate is "to rule or control; to exert the supreme determining or guiding influence on; to occupy the most prominent position in or over something."[1]

> **Intimidation:** To intimidate is "to make timid or fearful; to frighten; to discourage or suppress by threats or by violence."[2]

> **Manipulation:** To manipulate is "to handle or manage shrewdly and deviously for one's own profit."[3]

Again, there is no "preferred" method of control. And none of these components of control is in the nature of God. *God does not control; God reigns.* Controlling is not in Him; it is foreign to His very nature. Control stinks of satan. Control can't dance. Control is dry and unbaptized.

Confession: Good for the Soul and for Ammunition!

At this point, I need to make a confession. My greatest fear in writing this book is that some will use it to become better control-ites. I cringe at the thought that someone will read this book and then use it as a weapon against someone else: spouse, pastor, etc. I want to make it unmistakably clear that *no one is given permission to judge others on their control methods or habits!* We are human beings, not God. Only God can judge. In terms of repentance and restoration, we are responsible only for ourselves—no one else. Anyone who is not mature enough to leave the judging to God should throw the book away right now!

My fear about writing this book is not unfounded; I've learned it by experience. The week after I returned from Indiana, I preached a sermon on the subject of control as pictured in Rock/Paper/Scissors, and I have expanded and taught on the subject repeatedly ever since then. Without exception, someone has used the sermon against someone else, often against me. I have to admit that it cut to the quick to have someone I love, a church member, come up and accuse me of trying to manipulate situations in the church, using the line, "You've said yourself that you are a manipulator." I've learned, however, that such remarks go with the territory. Besides, trying to defend myself doesn't help much, either. Even so, I feel compelled to warn people up front not to use this material as a weapon. Furthermore, I feel the necessity of warning pastors and teachers that the teaching may be used against them. Perhaps there should be a warning label on this material:

*Warning teachers and preachers: Using this material **will** expose you to the control nature of others, especially as you confess your own weaknesses.*

More importantly, however, I need to remind readers, on the front end, of the amazing capacity of God to set us free from all the wickedness of our fallen nature, including control!

I have come to remind people, in no uncertain terms, that I am a *reformed* manipulator. I am a *former* manipulator. Does my old nature still surface from time to time? Sure! However, I'm not imprisoned by it anymore. "Manipulator" no longer defines me. I'm not proud of what I was; but, having been set free by the Lamb of God, I rejoice in Him! By the grace of God, I am not the person I used to be! If we really believe that God can and does heal alcoholics, sexual deviants, addicts, liars, cheats, partiers, jerks, and scum (such as some of us were) surely we can believe that He heals control freaks, such as all of us were (see 1 Cor. 6:11).

We are not talking, however, about superficial teaching or superficial healing. We are talking about *healing to the core!* To be a *former* dominator, manipulator, or intimidator requires the transformation of the very nature within us. Thank God that "what is impossible for man is possible with God!" (See Matthew 19:26.) We are transformed from glory to glory, as we behold Jesus (see 2 Cor. 3:18). We just need to behold Him so often that our very core being begins to look like Him "as in a mirror"!

Identifying the Nature Within

In my experience, I've found that most people are able to identify their own control techniques almost as soon as I begin to talk about the subject. However, because it may be helpful in our self-identification, I have prepared a table depicting what manipulators, dominators, and intimidators value most, as well as what they fear most. The table, however, should *not* be used to diagnose anyone other than self. It is presented only in the hope that, as we ponder the values and fears of the three types of controllers, we will begin to identify the patterns that have defined our lives and our interactions with others.

Control Type	Game Piece	Value Most	Fear Most
Dominator	Rock	Winning	Losing
Intimidator	Scissors	Being Right	Embarrassment
Manipulator	Paper	Acceptance	Conflict

As the table indicates, studies could be done on the interactions of, say, a dominating husband and a manipulating wife, or an intimidating boss with a dominating employee, *but that is beyond the focus of this book.* My prayer is that we will just look at ourselves and go to the *Fountain of Healing!*

Servant Ministry—Equipped Without Control!

So where does healing begin? As the Lord showed me that day in the car headed toward Muncie, it begins as we become more and more equipped to do ministry, growing up and not being "children tossed to and fro" (see Eph. 4:11-16). It is other's use of control that tends to toss us, and it is our attempts to control, rather than just be servants, that bind us to wallow in satan's nature. Equipped, however, *"for the work of ministry"* (Eph. 4:12), we move away from our inherent nature and move toward God's nature as we serve and as we *"grow up...into Him who is the head"* (Eph. 4:15).

The Greek word for "equip," as in *"for the equipping of the saints for the work of ministry"* (Eph. 4:12) is also translated "to mend." What a beautiful picture! True church leaders are empowered by Jesus to mend the saints so that they can do ministry, and it is in the doing of ministry that our fixation on controlling people and situations gives way to flowing in the nature of God! In fact, this mending, as in the "mending of nets," is the deep mending of our very nature, away from control and toward being the Body of Christ, *"knit together by what every joint supplies"* (Eph. 4:16).

When we are thus mended and knit together, the old nature of control is largely supplanted by a new nature, that of the ultimate Servant-Leader, Jesus. The game of Rock/Paper/Scissors gives way to something far more beautiful and precious, a life lived in mutual submission within the Body of Christ.

Giving up the game of control should settle something deep within us: servant ministry is not optional in the Kingdom of God. Mutual submission is not optional in the Kingdom of God. We are saved for good works (see Eph. 2:10). As Jesus through James reminds us, *"Faith without works is dead"* (James 2:26). Growing up into mature believers is not optional. Laying down our hell-bent nature to control others and every situation of life isn't optional! It (our control nature) may look like Rock/Paper/Scissors, but ultimately this isn't a game. Either we grow up, submit, and serve, or we will find ourselves being tossed to and fro until we haven't a clue as to who Jesus is or what true Christianity is all about.

Chapter Seven

THE SOURCE OF CONTROL

We don't know how long Adam and Eve enjoyed perfection in The Garden, we just know it wasn't long enough! Neither do we know how long satan had been a fallen and rebellious former angel before he approached Eve as "father of all lies." What we do know, however, is that satan's nature is the very opposite of God's. From the Fall, we also know that life is the opposite of death, that Heaven is the opposite of hell, and that dominion is the opposite of control.

God Reigns; Satan Controls

God *is* love, humility, and truth. Satan *operates in* domination, intimidation, and manipulation. God dances the perichoretic dance of perfect unity within the perfect Trinity; satan can't dance because all he wants to do is "lead," and that by control. Besides, he isn't a real trinity at all: he is just a fake, a usurper, a wannabe. The devil's lust for God's glory and divinity is so complete that he will cheat, lie, steal, destroy—anything to resemble (but only to those who like him are fallen and blind!) the Majesty who is God.

What is the source of control? Control is the outward manifestation of the entirely selfish, twisted, contorted "soul" of satan. Control is satan's "power" mechanism. It is how he rules this world.

How The Garden Became a Weed Patch...

The original creation must have been something to see. And something in which to live! It really boggles the mind when we glimpse into the pre-Fall realities: the original righteousness of Adam and Eve; the provision of all their needs (food, water, temperature, etc.); their perfect walk with God and each other; and a place where nothing marred the peace because animals, insects, and plants were in perfect relationship.

Everything was perfectly perfect! Everything looked like, acted like, loved like, shared like, gave like, cared like, and danced like God! The Garden was a picture of the perfect ontology (character/nature/being) of God. There was no shame, no fear, no hate, no death, no lies, no disunity, no sin, no satan—until Adam let down his guard.

Humans, of course, were created in God's image; so, in the beginning, we had His ontology as well. We were created tripartite beings as a reflection of the Triune God: we have a body, a soul, and a spirit. At first, all that we were "danced" perfectly with all that God is. Adam danced perfectly with Eve, and together they danced in perfect dominion over all the rest of creation.

As an angel, a spirit-being, lucifer lacked the triune fullness of humanity; and he didn't like that fact one bit. (In fact, it must have driven him insane!) On top of that, his worship of God, which had been so amazing at first, turned inward as he began to worship himself. (There is a lesson here for all of us!)

As we have already seen in Isaiah 14:12-17 and Ezekiel 28:11-19, lucifer rebelled; lucifer fell; lucifer decided to "be like God." But lacking divinity, he had (and has) to mimic all things triune. Lacking the righteous authority to reign like God, satan had to administer through control—domination, manipulation, and intimidation. No doubt, he was also irate over the change his fall had caused. Once breathtakingly beautiful, lucifer, the "anointed cherub," had become a "slithering snake." Talk about a fall!

...And How the Weed Patch Spread Inside Us

If only the fallen nature of satan had just stayed *with* and *in* satan! Sadly, satan was not the only one who fell from original beauty. Think about how beautiful Adam and Eve must have been before they fell! However, seduced into thinking they could be "like God," they fell, not only *away* from the character/nature of God, but *toward* the twisted mess lucifer had become. Genesis 3:1-7 give us an amazing picture not only of satan's ontology (vv. 1-5), but also of the *transfer* of his ontological distortion to humanity. The passage reads:

> *Now the serpent was more cunning than any beast of the field which the Lord God had made. And he said to the woman, "Has God indeed said, 'You shall not eat of every tree of the garden'?" And the woman said to the serpent, "We may eat the fruit of the trees of the garden; but of the fruit of the tree which is in the midst of the garden, God has said, 'You shall not eat it, nor shall you touch it, lest you die.'" Then the serpent said to the woman, "You will not surely die. For God knows that in the day you eat of it your eyes will be opened, and you will be like God, knowing good and evil." So when the woman saw that the tree was good for food, that it was pleasant to the eyes, and a tree desirable to make one wise, she took of its fruit and ate. She also gave to her husband with her, and he ate. Then the eyes of both of them were opened, and they knew that they were naked; and they sewed fig leaves together and made themselves coverings* (Genesis 3:1-7).

Note that satan, operating out of his own being, used *domination* ("you will not surely die"), *manipulation* ("Has God indeed said?"), and *intimidation* ("you will be like God") to entice Eve. It is intriguing to see how quickly the nature of control transferred to Eve. Having been controlled through domination, she is now seeing and thinking like a dominator: she decided that *"the tree was good for food."* It's as if she thought, "That fruit looks good and, doggone it, I'm going to take me some!" Then, seeing through the eyes of a manipulator, she recognized that the tree was *"pleasant to the eyes."* It's as if Eve, just wanting to slip something by quickly and painlessly, said, "Wow, that sure is pretty. I'll just sneak me a bite." Next, seeing through the eyes of an intimidator, she believed that the tree would make her wise. It's as if Eve, longing for the wisdom of God and its accompanying power, said, "I **will** be right, I **will** be wise; now give me some fruit!"

The crowning picture of this scenario in Eden is that Adam and Eve used fig leaves to try and cover their nakedness. As stated before, ancient Jewish scholars believed that the tree of the knowledge of good and evil was a fig tree and that Adam and Eve just reached out and took leaves from the tree in front of them to make their tunics. They dressed themselves in the Fall! They dressed in *control!* Because they had dressed themselves in the ontology of satan, their very first act was an attempt to control the disaster they had caused. Because of this transfer of darkness, all of Adam and Eve's progeny come into the world dressed in the same ontology. All humans are born dressed in *original sin!*

Jesus alluded to this transfer when He spoke to the Jews about *"My Father"* and *"your father"* in John 8:38. On the heels of that statement, He declared to them the identity of their father:

> *You are of your father the devil, and the desires of your father*
> *you want to do. He was a murderer from the beginning, and*
> *does not stand in the truth, because there is no truth in him.*
> *When he speaks a lie, he speaks from his own resources, for he is*
> *a liar and the father of it* (John 8:44).

Although these particular Jews believed in Jesus (see John 8:31), they were acting out of the nature of their father, satan, whose transfer of darkness in Eden had been passed down to them. By extension, what Jesus said to these Jews can be said of all of us. In our fallen state, our father is satan, the murderer and liar; and we are like him. We, like satan, speak from his resources—fallen, devoid-of-truth lies.

The crowd Jesus was speaking to, when confronted with (and by) the truth, reacted in a completely normal and predictable way: they drew within themselves and their natural "resources." They got more religious, belligerent, and rebellious. They wanted to control the situation and their level of discomfort, even if it meant stoning the Son of God! (See John 8:59.) We humans, like our father the devil, are nothing if not predictable!

But There Is Good News

The good news is that in Jesus, we become prone, by grace, to live in original righteousness again! We live now in the absolute hope and knowledge that original righteousness eventually will be perfectly restored, with every hint of the Fall—satan, his personality, and our absorbing of it—gone!

Clearly, the source of control is satan. As a result of his fall, lucifer became monstrously deformed. In that form, he entered Eden and used his warped nature to entice Eve to deception and Adam to rebellion. Then, in their Fall, they took on satan's monstrous nature, which is passed down to all humans.

However, there was, and is, hope! Because God created us as a trinity, there would be, through Him, a way of escape from our fallen state. We may be totally depraved, but we're not totally without hope. If God could just provide a way for our *spirit* to be justified, declared and made not guilty—if God could just provide a way for our *soul* (mind/will/emotions) to be progressively regenerated and made holy, from glory to glory—if God could just provide a way for us to receive a new *body*, free from ravages of the Fall. *"Oh the blood of Jesus, it washes white as snow!"*

Chapter Eight

THE BREADTH OF CONTROL

There was a hilarious commercial based on the Rock/Paper/Scissors game that I saw while watching the 2007 Super Bowl. It was a beer commercial (why does the beer industry have all the best ads?) in which two guys are fighting over the last bottle of beer in a tub of ice. One suggests to the other that they play Rock/Paper/Scissors to decide who gets the last beer. As they are playing, one suddenly drops to the ground as if knocked down and almost knocked out by something. The one on the ground shouts, "But I threw paper!" To which the other, with the cold beer in hand, replies, "And I *threw* a rock."

The commercial serves to show, in a comical way, just how wicked our control nature can be. We'll even cheat at Rock/Paper/Scissors if it will get us our way! In addition to being an example of the extent of the game of control in contemporary society, it reflects a pattern of control seen repeatedly in Scripture.

Over the years, I have been amazed at how often I have seen in Scripture the triune appearance of domination/manipulation/ intimidation. Over and over again, I've noticed the devil's nature operating in human beings, implied in some instances but, in others, quite clearly defined within the text. Nehemiah struggled against Sanballet the dominator, Geshem the intimidator, and Tobiah the manipulator as they teamed up to use all three methods of control against him. Ezra dealt with unnamed controlling adversaries. Pharaoh tried to dominate Moses; Goliath intimidated all of Israel's army (except David); and Delilah manipulated Samson. While there are many more examples, I have prepared a table to illustrate the breadth of control from Genesis to Revelation.

Sometimes, the picture is quite startling, as with the three temptations of Christ in the wilderness. The pattern of temptation satan used with Jesus was a virtual copy of what he did in The Garden. Of course! Since satan is what he is, he can't help being predictable in and to his own nature. On the other hand, Jesus, operating from His own ontology, deflected and rejected all of satan's temptations. Because He was fully human, He was just as tempted and just as vulnerable as Adam. The temptations, of physical hunger, of no-cost rule, of personal pride and position, were very real. Yet *because he is a man of perfect character*, Jesus did not fall for satan's lies.

Control Type	Realm of Attack	Satan's Fall *Ezek. 28: 16-17*	First Temptation *Gen. 3:1-5*	Transfer *Gen. 3:6-7*	Temptation of Christ *Luke 4:1-13*
Domination	Physical (Body)	Wealth: "filled with violence"	"You will not surely die."	"The tree was good for food…"	"Command this stone to become bread."
Manipulation	Emotional (Soul)	Corrupt wisdom: "your splendor"	"Has God indeed said…?"	"It was pleasant to the eyes…"	"The devil… showed Him all the kingdoms…"
Intimidation	Spiritual (Spirit)	Heart pride: "your beauty"	"You will be like God…"	"A tree desirable to make one wise…"	"Throw Yourself down from here."

Sometimes the picture of control in Scripture is quite subtle, as in the final temptation of Christ in the Garden of Gethsemane, which Scripture simply speaks of as "this cup" (see Matt. 26; Luke 22). Matthew records that Jesus three times prayed that, if possible, "this cup" would be removed from Him. It also records the disciples' ontological response of falling asleep each time Jesus went aside to pray (see Matt. 26; Mark 14). While some speculation is necessary here, it seems plausible that Jesus was once more and once-and-for-all faced with control's temptations to manipulate or dominate or intimidate Him out of death on the cross. On the other hand, operating still from their fallen self-being, the disciples just *controlled* the situation by sleeping. (Denial is a powerful form of manipulation!)

At other times, however, the scriptural picture brings clarity and definition to a scriptural concept, as in seeing the correlation of the three types of control with each part of our triune nature:

Final Temptation *Matt. 26: 36-46*	Works of Flesh *Gal. 5:16-24*	The World *1 John 2:16*	False Teachers *Jude 11*	In the Church *Rev. 2*	Final Battle *Rev. 16:13*
"This cup"... ...*Asleep*	"Selfish ambition"	"The lust of the flesh"	"The way of Cain"	"Doctrine of the Nicolaitans"	the dragon (satan)
"This cup"... ...*Asleep*	"Discord dissensions, factions" (NIV)	"The lust of the eyes"	"The error of Balaam"	"Doctrine of Balaam"	the beast (antichrist)
"This cup"... ...*Asleep*	"Fits of rage; hatred" (NIV)	"The pride of life"	"The rebellion of Korah"	"That woman Jezebel...a prophetess"	The false prophet

(1) "The lust of the flesh": domination in the physical realm,

(2) "The lust of the eyes": manipulation in the soulish realm, and

(3) "The pride of life": intimidation in the spiritual realm.

Because we are triune beings, we are vulnerable to demonic attack in each of these three areas, and we operate in a fallen way in each of these three areas.

Sometimes, seeing this repeated pattern of control in Scripture is important to understanding what the Lord is saying through a passage, as in his tripartite warning to the Church of every age and location through His letters to the seven churches in the book of Revelation. When Jesus spoke of the "doctrine of the Nicolaitans," we need to grasp the fact that He was referring to the *domination* of the laity: literally *Nicolaitans* means "conquering the laity." When He referred to the "doctrine of Balaam," He was speaking of *manipulation*, alluding to the fact that when Balaam could not directly curse Israel, he brought destruction via the back door, enticement to harlotry with the women of Moab. When He referred to "that prophetess Jezebel," He was speaking of *intimidation*, which Jezebel used to control Ahab, and even Elijah, into submission. Seeing this correlation surely helps us more fully grasp Jesus' warning to the churches—then and now.

A Scripture reference that reinforces the fact that Jesus' reference to Jezebel was referring to intimidation is First Kings 21:25, which reads:

> *But there was no one like Ahab who sold himself to do wickedness in the sight of the Lord, because Jezebel his wife stirred* [incited] *him up.*

This "stirring" destroyed Ahab and made Elijah run and hide like a scared child. Jezebel was no slick manipulator; she was just one scary, intimidating lady!

Hopefully, it should also be obvious that intimidation is a human-nature problem, not a female problem. The "Jezebel spirit" is certainly found in men, probably more often than in women. Intimidation, like domination and manipulation, isn't gender sensitive: it's just fallen and demonic.

Also important in seeing this repeated biblical pattern is the recognition that, while we humans may have the ability to use all three control methods to get our way, most of us have a "preferred" method. Like the Nicolaitans, some of us tend to be dominators. Like Balaam, some of us tend to be manipulators. And like Jezebel, some of us tend to be intimidators. All of us operate out of a primary control mechanism and method, unless, in our frenzy to get our own way and to "be like God," we momentarily switch to another method for the "need" of the moment. Soon enough, however, we revert to the method that works "best" for us.

Finally, perhaps most importantly in these last days, there is a necessity of seeing the personification of control through the manifestation of satan's false trinity. Revelation 16:13 reads:

> *And I saw three unclean spirits like frogs coming out of the mouth of the dragon, out of the mouth of the beast, and out of the mouth of the false prophet.*

The dragon, the beast, and the false prophet all personify an aspect of satan's full nature. The beast (antichrist) personifies *manipulation*; the dragon, *domination*; and the false prophet, *intimidation*. The dragon, of course, is actually satan; and he is unipersonal, not tripartite like God and humanity. Limited to his non-triune nature, he will have to employ two humans, the antichrist and the false prophet to mimic and blaspheme God. Through these "puppets" he will personify the full extent of his fallen control nature. Each area of satan's controlling nature is a realm of demonic activity, as indicated by John's description in Revelation 16:13.

Satan's "trinity" is frightful and powerful! It is the ultimate mocking of the glorious nature (ontology) of Almighty God. Yet as we endure the shaking and refining in these days of the "labor pains," let us remember that the true Trinity of God will triumph over the false trinity of the devil. The dominion and sovereignty of the Most High will destroy the control of the "most low"!

From Genesis to Revelation, the pattern of control appears over and over again, illustrating the great "breadth" of control; but (Hallelujah!) we see a far greater breadth to the glory and grace of Christ Jesus the Lord, such breadth that one day (soon!), all that is control will be forever gone!

Chapter Nine

THE OPPOSITE OF CONTROL

In order to better understand control, we need to recognize and celebrate its opposite. The credit for this thought goes to a phone call I received from a farmer friend from Kentucky. He is one of those people who is able to hear and see the Lord in almost every circumstance of life. The day he called, he'd been out on his tractor on a cold, rainy day after a period of hard-freezing weather. Because the ground was so hard-frozen that the rain only made it slick and dangerous, my friend had slipped in the tractor over a hill. "It's raining on frozen ground," he said when he called. And, for once, I was the one who saw the spiritual implication of his conversation.

Frozen ground, I realized, is an apt description of the human condition. Although the Latter Rain is falling upon us, it can only make us *slick and dangerous*, unless and until we *thaw out* enough to allow the *Rain* to soak into us. One way of melting that *ice of control* in us is to understand the opposite of control. The warmth of God's *Rain* will melt our hearts if we really understand the antonyms of domination, intimidation, and manipulation.

Antonyms of Control—in Word and Deed

If we look up the antonyms (opposites) of the word *domination*, we'll find words like "compliance" and "submission." Another word that summarizes the opposite of domination is the word *Love*. Love, of course, is who God is, all of Him. The apostle John specifically uses the word *love* in describing the Father (see 1 John 4:8).

If we look up the antonyms of the word *intimidation*, we will find words such as "calm," "encourage," and "praise." A great summary word for these terms is the word *humility*. Although this term is descriptive of all of the Godhead, the author of Philippians (God, through Paul) specifically applies it to the Son, Jesus (see Phil. 2 NIV).

If we look up the antonyms of the word *manipulation*, you'll find words like "protect," "advise," or "guard." Here, the best summary word is *truth*, which, of course, is descriptive of the very nature of all of the Godhead. Both Isaiah and the psalmist used the epithet *"God of truth"* (Ps. 31:5; Isa. 65:16). The apostle John specifically applies the term *truth* to the Holy Spirit (see 1 John 5:6).

Love. Humility. Truth. These three cannot capture all of who God is, but they certainly capture everything control is not. It helps to recognize in these three simple realities how very different the being of God is from the being of satan or humans. Surely, a very large part of our redemption lies in our moving progressively and definitively away from domination *toward love;* away from intimidation *toward humility;* and away from manipulation *toward truth.* And in addition to giving us word pictures and opposites to ponder, Scripture also presents the way of living opposite to control.

Under Authority and Out of Control

Remember the centurion who demonstrated great faith to Jesus? Matthew 8:8-13 reads:

> *The centurion answered and said, "Lord, I am not worthy that You should come under my roof. But only speak a word, and my servant will be healed. For I also am a man under authority, having soldiers under me. And I say to this one, 'Go,' and he goes; and to another, 'Come,' and he comes; and to my servant, 'Do this,' and he does it." When Jesus heard it, He marveled, and said to those who followed, "Assuredly, I say*

to you, I have not found such great faith, not even in Israel! And I say to you that many will come from east and west, and sit down with Abraham, Isaac, and Jacob in the kingdom of heaven. But the sons of the kingdom will be cast out into outer darkness. There will be weeping and gnashing of teeth." Then Jesus said to the centurion, "Go your way; and as you have believed, so let it be done for you." And his servant was healed that same hour.

"A man under authority!" Here, we have the key words. It is impossible to be *in* authority unless and until one is *under* authority. Said another way, only when people are *under* authority do they *have* true authority. Jesus has *all* authority because He is perfectly under authority.

Control is an attempt to usurp authority, as modeled by satan. Control, then, is the attempt to *have* authority without being *under* authority! When we understand this fact, we begin to understand why it is so important to submit ourselves to the authority of those whom God has placed over us. There is protection in being under authority. There is true authority in being under authority. Apart from being properly submitted under godly authority, there is nothing but control-ism.

The centurion's encounter with Jesus clearly shows the opposite, the spiritual antonym, of *control* is "submission." We are in a place where control gives way to authority when we are submitted to those in authority over us, and mutually submitted *"in the fear of God"* to those around us in the Church (see Eph. 5:21). Unfortunately, however, our control nature has a real problem with submission, with being under authority! Our basic human nature, our satanic ontology, abhors the whole concept! We like being the boss; we like playing God. This fact is why the centurion's attitude shocked and blessed Jesus so much. Again, unfortunately, the centurion's attitude is just about as rare in "Israel after the Spirit" (the Church) today as it was in "Israel after the flesh" on that day! Let it never be forgotten that it is our very being, our fallen nature, our warped ontology, that battles against submission. Remembering that fact should give us courage to tell our flesh, our natural self, to shut up!

Fortunately, Scripture is full of examples of those who have been transformed by the grace of our Lord Jesus. These were those who discovered by the revelation of God the opposite of control. These were those who were fully "wet" with God, thus equipped to battle the fallen nature within. These were those who walked under authority, thus walking in authority, not control. These were those who chose to serve, not be served. These people, after Jesus got hold of them, exhibited truth, love, and humility rather than domination, intimidation, or manipulation.

Paul, Peter, and James are three outstanding scriptural examples of transformation *away from* a controlling nature *toward* a godly nature. To illustrate these transformations, I have prepared the table on the facing page.

Note that two of the three had a name change. Simon's name change is quite interesting. *Simon* means "hear me," while *Peter* means "the little rock." When Jesus was trying to get Peter to listen, even after He renamed him Peter, Jesus used the name Simon. *"Simon, Simon! Indeed Satan has asked for you, that he may sift you as wheat"* (Luke 22:31). Jesus wanted to make sure he was listening! But after his sifting and restoration and empowerment with the Holy Spirit, Peter indeed became the "rock" who was faithful—even, if tradition is correct, to being crucified upside down. Obviously, Peter's highest value in life shifted from being *accepted* to being *faithful*. While his manipulative ways are pretty easy to see early on, Simon the "paper" became quite a "rock" (but not a dominator!) later on. God transformed this former "kiss up" manipulator into a mighty apostle and pastor. Former manipulators make loving and powerful pastors *in the Lord!*

Saul became Paul. The significance of this name change is found in the fact that Saul was a Jewish name, while Paul was a Greek name. Saul, the highly trained Jewish religionist became Paul, the apostle to the Greeks. Although Paul did give up on "religiosity," it was not at the expense of his rich Jewish roots. God built upon that firm foundation, thereby giving Paul supreme authority in arguing that the Judaizers were wrong in attempting to force that "old-time religion" on Gentile believers. Tragically, however, the Church later caused great pain and division by forcing Jews to give up their identity to become Christians.

Control Type	Unredeemed Examples	Most Valued:	Key Scriptures	Changed by:	Redeemed by Grace:	New Value:	Perfected By:
Domination	Saul (Religiously bound)	Winning	Acts 9:1-30	Love	Paul (Apostle to the Greeks)	Finishing	"love your enemies" Matt. 5:44
Manipulation	Simon "Hear Me"	Being Accepted	Matt. 16: 13-23 John 21	Truth	Peter "Little rock"	Being Faithful	"made perfect in one" John 17:23
Intimidation	James, unbelieving half-brother to Jesus in the flesh	Being Right	John 7:3-4 1 Cor. 15:7	Humility	James, Apostle: Full-brother to Jesus by the Spirit	Being Godly	"a perfect man, able...to bridle" James 3:2

Paul, though, was transformed away from the dominating nature that was so obvious in his early life as Saul. While he valued "winning" as he was imprisoning and terrifying Christians, he came to value "finishing" as his character changed from control to submission. In fact, Paul could point to "finishing well" (see 2 Tim. 4:7-8) as the mighty epitaph to his life on earth in the Lord. Former dominators make great leaders and church-planting apostles, *in the Lord!*

Although James' name didn't change, his character surely did! While Jesus was his half-brother, James remained a decidedly sidelined non-believer until Jesus' resurrection. (Family members are always the hardest to witness to!) Early in James' life, being right seemed to be the thing he valued most (see John 7:3-5); but, soaked in the humility which is God, James' values changed. He came to value *being godly*, being a doer of the Word, more than *being right*. James had been such an intimidator early in life that he impacted most of his family's opinion about Jesus. However, James the intimidator became James the teacher. Former intimidators make great teaching pastors and apostles, *in the Lord!*

The main point to all these examples is the promise and reality that we humans can change—dramatically and to the very core of our being—through the transforming grace of Jesus Christ. Our values change. Control gives way to operating in godly authority. And in Heaven, if not on earth, our name even changes! (See Revelation 2:17.)

There is no such thing as sinless control by domination/intimidation/manipulation. Through these efforts to be "like God," we are manifesting the ontology of satan. On the other hand, we are manifesting the ontology of Jesus when we submit to His Lordship, *putting off* our "old man" and *putting on* Jesus Christ (see Rom. 13:14). Simons become Peters, Sauls become Pauls, and Jameses finally become real brothers!

What About Using Control to Accomplish Good?

Sooner or later, certain questions regarding the matter of control will be asked: "What about using control to accomplish *good*? What about the ends justifying the means? Doesn't the generosity of certain millionaires outweigh their slightly naughty means?" To those questions, we have to admit that history is replete with tyrannical leaders who nonetheless did many good things. Through the force of their controlling personalities, they built armies and cities and aqueducts and highways and libraries and hospitals. We also have to admit that even in our congregations we have not-so-tyrannical leaders who seem to love the Lord although they are leading from a place of dominating, or manipulating, or intimidating. Our tendency is to overlook, perhaps even celebrate, the millionaire who builds us a new sanctuary, or purchases a new parsonage, or does whatever out of his control nature while secretly desiring a big brass plaque to honor him for his efforts.

The truth is that, with our fallen knowledge, we are capable of doing a lot of "good," of controlling people and events with the effect of building sanctuaries and aqueducts and highways and libraries; however, the "good" is still sin. It is fruit from the *wrong tree!* We must never forget that the tree of the knowledge of good and evil was the *wrong tree.* The tree of life accomplishes great and perfect good—without ever resorting to domination, intimidation, or manipulation. Control is simply not found in God. There is no such thing as "godly control"; hence, giving away millions to charity does not justify the giver if he acquired his fortune by trampling others down through intimidation, domination, or manipulation, or if the gift itself is an act of control! Although we may suggest that the *ends* justify the *means,* we are only justifying control!

Control has an opposite, the perfect authority and dominion of God. We were born to control, but we can and must be *reborn* to authority and dominion. The great good news is that, in Jesus, we can expect a change that is so deep, so transforming, that we actually interact with people in a whole new way, with love and humility and truth—in authority, rather than the old ways of domination, intimidation, and manipulation—in control.

No church, no Christian, and no pastor should ever settle for less than this great transformation in Jesus, even if millions of dollars and the potential for some *powerful* disgruntled members are on the line! And quite inversely, we can never expect the transforming grace of God to operate in our churches if we are knowingly operating from the wrong tree for the sake of money or "peace" in the pews. We must confront control, and we must expect transformation!

Chapter Ten

OVERCOMING CONTROL

A s a pastor, I have had the privilege of watching people go from being non-Christians, to being "baby" Christians, to being fully mature Christians. Watching that progression from birth to full adulthood is the *most satisfying* aspect of my ministry. However, seeing that progression interrupted and short-circuited is the *most common* aspect of my ministry. I suspect this disappointment is true for most pastors. No doubt, the reality is that most of our churches are populated by believers who, in Jesus, possess unlimited potential for growth although in practice they often experience remarkably limited growth.

One problem in evangelical circles is that we have taken one extremely slim slice of the "Gospel pie"—going to Heaven—and made it the whole thing. Millions of believers basically think that the only goal is to "get saved,"

and...

then...

wait...

to...

die (and go to Heaven!).

We have reduced the Gospel to a few spiritual laws and taught our congregations to think this way! Our goal, to make the Gospel simple and easy to swallow, was not necessarily wrong; however, the result has been chronic immaturity. In some circles, the Gospel pie has been reduced to other slim slices, like mandatory speaking in tongues, or being baptized a certain way, or showing up at church once in a while. The fact is that reduction of the Gospel in any way only produces retardation of maturity among the saints.

One of the most amazing things about maturity in the faith is that it is not so much about the length of time one has been a believer as about the obedience, submission, and surrender of the believer. Consequently, most churches have a few young saints, even teenagers, who walk in great spiritual maturity, and a few 90-year-olds who just don't. Age alone is not the deciding factor: repeatedly "beholding the Lord as in a mirror" is! (See Second Corinthians 3:18.)

Of course, an octogenarian who has lived a life in the Word and by the Holy Spirit submitted in loving ministry is a beautiful saint to behold! My heart cry is for *all* the folks in my church to want to grow like that, to be remarkably mature as a twenty-year-old, becoming a Billy Graham or a Mother Teresa in their later years. The early Methodists called this process "going on to perfection," and a few of us are still crazy enough as to think that a "big slice" point is that we become so much like the Lord in a life given over to Him that we live like, love like, heal like, deliver like, serve like, and smell like Jesus in the here and now!

The sad truth, however, is that most modern Methodists (and Baptists and Pentecostals and Catholics and Lutherans and Emergents and house church advocates and…) seem up to the task, as long as it doesn't require more than an hour or so (90 minutes for Pentecostals) on Sunday mornings, and doesn't otherwise interfere with "life." God offers a walk; we want a momentary encounter. God offers a relationship; we want a religion. God offers the whole Gospel pie; we want a tiny slice to call our own.

Regretfully, we have a desperate need for maturity in the Body of Christ, and an absolute epidemic of immaturity. Obedience and submission are needed. Transformation is needed. Healing and deliverance are needed. Surely, all this grace should and must impact the way we interact with people. Surely, our very nature, all the way down to control, should and must be changed! But this change isn't a fruit of immaturity. Mature fruit can be produced only by mature disciples. Deep inner transformation of our control core requires a level of maturity that many believers are either unaware of, or are unwilling to seek and behold.

Overcomer—Or Just Overwhelmed?

We have already looked at the passage from Revelation 12:7-12 which describes those believers throughout the ages who overcome satan by *"the blood of the Lamb"* and by *"the word of their testimony,"* and because *"they did not love their lives to the death."* We have already seen that this is not only a powerful general statement of a disciple's ability to overcome the devil, but that it also has a very specific meaning in terms of the control nature. To summarize:

- Satan cannot *manipulate* believers who know who they are by and in the blood of Jesus. The doorway of manipulation is closed when we know that our past is forgiven; that our weaknesses are redeemed; and that our shame and guilt are covered by God's *Tunic of Skin*. Confidence in what was accomplished on the cross gives believers victory over emotional attacks. How can the accuser charge a believer with what the blood has cleansed? Also, because the blood is "of sin the double cure," the *compulsion to manipulate others* fades away in the disciple's life!

- Satan cannot *intimidate* disciples who have a testimony alive by the Word, and who aren't afraid to share it. When a follower of Christ has a story of transformation to tell, the very act of telling it increases faith and diminishes satan's ability to bring down, frighten, and generally cut up a believer. A testimony of transformation closes the door on *spiritual* attacks. Furthermore, as believers share their stories of God's grace, their *compulsion to intimidate others* fades away!

- Finally, satan cannot *dominate* those who have already given their lives away. When the fear of physical death is replaced by a deep love for Jesus that transcends death and an absolute assurance of His victory over death, then satan loses his ability to attack us in the physical realm. Truly, this is winning by dying to self! When disciples love Jesus more than life itself, they find Life Himself, and the *compulsion to dominate others* fades away!

Satan controls by manipulating, intimidating, and dominating. In a far too similar fashion, so do humans. However, when a believer's *past* is washed by the blood, when the *present* is a living testimony of the Word, and when the *future* is safe by loving Jesus more than life, satan loses his control over that believer. By laying down his "right" to control other people, a believer is a shining example of "Overcoming Christianity!"

When physical, emotional, and spiritual entry points are closed, satan is overcome. When past, present, and future are safely buried in Christ, satan is overcome. And, when satan is overcome in a person's life, the tendency to act like him is progressively overcome. The *"ruler of this world"* could find *"nothing in"* Jesus (John 14:30)—nothing in his past, present, or future by which to attack Him; nothing physically, emotionally, or spiritually that gave satan a foothold; and nothing in the way of domination, intimidation, or manipulation to control by or through. This kind of submission is the perfection that is Jesus, and this is the perfection that every believer should desire, an "overcoming" perfection that shuts the door on the devil and opens the door to treating neighbors in Christlike, control-less love.

Grownup, or Control-ite?

So is this "perfection" (maturity) automatic? No! Paul explained this fact to his flock at Corinth in a startlingly clear way in First Corinthians 2:13–3:4:

> *These things we also speak, not in words which man's wisdom teaches but which the Holy Spirit teaches, comparing spiritual*

things with spiritual. But the natural man does not receive the things of the Spirit of God, for they are foolishness to him; nor can he know them, because they are spiritually discerned. But he who is spiritual judges all things, yet he himself is rightly judged by no one. For "who has known the mind of the Lord that he may instruct Him?" But we have the mind of Christ. And I, brethren, could not speak to you as to spiritual people but as to carnal, as to babes in Christ. I fed you with milk and not with solid food; for until now you were not able to receive it, and even now you are still not able; for you are still carnal. For where there are envy, strife, and divisions among you, are you not carnal and behaving like mere men? For when one says, "I am of Paul," and another, "I am of Apollos," are you not carnal?

Because the *"natural man"* is not saved, he can't receive the things of God. In the natural, humans have the nature, character, and resources of satan. We have his fallen nature.

The carnal person is a baby in Christ. Babies in Christ are immature believers, regardless of their chronological age or the number of years they have been followers. Although they are "saved," they still think like natural men and women. Their character and nature is still basically like satan's. Hence, they produce the fruit of division, envy, and strife.

The spiritual person is a mature believer who has the mind of Christ. Having the mind of Christ precludes having the character of satan! These are true disciples of Jesus Christ. These are the true "sons" of God, not just the "children" (see Romans 8). These are the ones who overcome satan! And the overcoming, spiritual Christianity is *normal* Christianity!

We should never pretend that being carnal is good enough. We should never pretend that a stunted, strife-filled, divisive Christianity should somehow be called normal. It is a travesty to pretend that control-ism is just fine and dandy in the Church! Natural and even carnal persons are still *bound* to act like the devil, which is why they should never be serving in leadership, and why that kind of behavior should never be glamorized or excused by Christian leaders!

We could never picture the apostle Paul celebrating the control-freak mentality of Corinth instead of correcting it. Then why do we in the modern Church so often celebrate it? Is a mega-sized congregation a valid excuse for tolerating a dominating pastor? Is a million dollar gift enough to justify an intimidating church person? Can we really overlook master manipulators simply because they "do such a good job with the children's department"? Of course not! God's expectation that we grow up, and quickly, to become spiritual, overcoming disciples hasn't changed a bit. His aversion to control-induced division, strife, and envy hasn't changed, either. But by His grace, we can change, and become overcomers!

Growing up in the Lord is nonnegotiable! Scripture speaks about it in various ways, all of which paint a compelling picture. Like John the Baptist, we can address it in terms of our decreasing, in order for Jesus to increase in our lives (see John 3:30). Like Peter, we can talk about the progression which begins with faith, but adds to it virtue (power), knowledge, self-control, and perseverance until one walks in brotherly kindness and love (see 2 Peter 1:5-7). We can use the language of Revelation 12, of being overcomers. We can use the imagery of First Corinthians 2 and 3 in terms of being spiritual Christians. We can challenge folks to *"go on to perfection"* (Heb. 6:1; see also Heb. 5:12–6:3) like the writer of Hebrews and the early Methodists did. We can differentiate between the works of the flesh and the fruit of the Spirit (see Gal. 5:16-26). There are many more examples, but only one expectation, that we grow up into Him who is the Head of the Body, Christ Jesus! (See Ephesians 4:7-16.)

Obviously, this growing up, if it is real, will involve a laying down of control-ism. Submission will be indicative of all relationships. Servant ministry will define motive and actions. The Holy Spirit will flow through like a river. Jesus will be easy to see. Milk will be replaced by meat. And the urge to dominate, intimidate, or manipulate will recede as our nature is progressively refined. The more we reflect Jesus, as in a mirror (see 2 Cor. 3:18), the less we will reflect satan. The more we have the mind and character of Christ, the less we'll think and bully like satan! Maturity in Jesus will allow us to overcome satan, including his methods of mimicking God!

Chapter Eleven

THE END OF CONTROL

The Bible begins with original perfection, and it ends with perfection restored.

All is well and wonderful in the first two chapters of Genesis and in the last two chapters of Revelation. However, these four chapters are the only chapters of Scripture that don't deal with satan, his fall, and our falling into his nature. Everything between Genesis 1 and 2 and Revelation 21 and 22 deals with the Fall, its costs, and the incredible lengths God has gone to so that we can move toward perfection now and live and reign in it in eternity. Every one of these other chapters somehow relates to the passion of our "dancing God" to restore His highest creation, His tripartite creation, to a place of perfect intimacy, perfect relationship, *perfect dance*, with and in Him!

Yes, perfection will be restored; and when it is restored, all vestige of control will be long gone. We will *reign* with Him forever and ever and it will be a true reign in perfect unity with the Godhead. Control, the imperfect attempt to rule apart from God, will no longer be in the picture.

Finally "Getting" the Kingdom

I first grasped the magnitude and importance of thinking in Kingdom terms while attending the second of the three week-long sessions on pastoral leadership taught by Dr. Jack Hayford as part of the doctoral program at The King's Seminary in October of 2005. I had chosen to go to The King's in order to sit under Dr. Hayford's teaching, and I certainly was not disappointed.

As well as being great teaching, Dr. Hayford's second-week teaching on the present and future reality of the Kingdom of God was also a time of *revelation* with God unfolding Scriptures and Kingdom concepts to me. Although I had preached on the Kingdom of God prior to this time, I honestly had not ever really grasped the magnitude and importance of thinking in Kingdom terms. The Lord greatly expanded my view of His Kingship, and the *present* reality of it, along with expanding my understanding of what He is doing in the *now*. That week changed my life, and I shall be eternally thankful that the Lord led me to The King's Seminary.

I went home to Tennessee awakened to an exciting, holistic understanding of God and His purposes. The *Kingdom* changed me. I spent the entire next year (2006) preaching on the Kingdom of God. The Lord led me and the church I serve through some fundamental changes. I began to understand and to preach and lead with Kingdom purposes in mind. We are to *be* the Kingdom, not just talk about it. We are to *release* Heaven around us, not just talk about going there someday!

Dr. Hayford spoke to us about three great C's, based on Matthew 16:13-21: the great *confession,* the great *conception,* and the great *commission.* The great confession, of course, is Peter's declaration of verse 16: *"You are the Christ, the Son of the living God."* In those great revelational moments when Peter first realized who Jesus is, a great *shift* occurred as Jesus explained that the Kingdom of God had invaded the world through His coming and that the Kingdom would continue to infiltrate and leaven the world through His Body, the Church. Jesus made clear to Peter that his confession had come from God the Father, not from "flesh and blood." This same confession, coming from God, not man (from *revelation*, not *information*), is the defining confession of the true Church always. The *great conception* Hayford spoke about is that Jesus conceived (and conceives) of His Church in victory, a Church entrusted with the *"keys of the kingdom of heaven"* (Matt. 16:19); a Church empowered by His Spirit to change the world; and a Church assured that "the gates of hell" could not prevail against it (see Matt. 16:18). Lastly, the *great commission* is to accomplish Christ's purposes on earth by binding and loosing, i.e., unleashing heaven amongst all the hell around us (see Matt. 16:19).

On January 1, 2006, I used the three greats—confession, conception, and commission, as the framework for the first sermon in a series I *knew* would encompass the entire year. Although I did not know exactly what the sermons would be, I was sure they would come. And come they did in what was an amazing season for me and my church as, week after week, Scripture after Scripture, parable after parable, the present reality of the Kingdom came alive to me and to many within my congregation. What an invigorating year of revelation and confirmation that was!

We, the Church, are empowered, equipped, and expected to do the King's work in preparation for His return. We, the Church, are His army; and we are responsible for releasing His grace and goodness while operating behind enemy lines. Our King has called us to a great work, and it is in the here and now!

Although having the sermons come from divine download week by week was a terrific blessing to me, I soon realized that my real Kingdom call was to shepherd the church through some essential changes in order for us to move away from being comfortable spectators of the Kingdom to being active participants in it, *commissioned* with authority, guided by what Jesus *conceives* for us to be, and grounded in the revelatory *confession* that Jesus is the Christ, the Son of the living God.

Because change is just plain hard for all of us, I knew that shepherding my church through the needed changes would not be an easy path, even with a great congregation of people who display a genuinely loving spirit and a significant maturity in the Lord. Change challenges control; it makes us feel that we are losing control. Thus, the tendency in even the best of us is to resist change until we realize that *losing control* can be a good thing once we grasp what control really is and from whence it comes. Consequently, carrying out my Kingdom call to effect change was not without some pronounced struggles.

Kingdom Changes—Needed More Than Wanted!

One of the changes involved worship music, an issue that has plagued many a congregation. Typically, we had two distinctly different services, one "traditional," and one "contemporary." What we really had, however, was two *de facto* congregations with little unity overall. I'm sure I don't need to spell it out, but one of the services tended to breed some spiritual arrogance while the other seemed to foster a complacent and even stubborn spirit. Since our Kingdom directive is to restore unity, we blended both services, having both services in the sanctuary, blending the worship band with the choir, and using both hymns and praise choruses in each service.

The initial result, of course, was to tick everyone off! One group thought I had "lost the Spirit"; the other thought that I was trying to cram "that new stuff" down their throats. The long-term Kingdom result, however, has been compromise, humility, and greater unity. The church segregated by musical preferences, age, economic status, race, or anything else simply is not the Kingdom in the fullest sense. Separation is just a result of control; unity requires the supernatural presence of God Himself!

The second major change, again brought about by a deep sense of Kingdom necessity (and confirmed by other leaders in the Body), was to change our corporate prayer time from monologue to prayer within small groups. Like most churches, our prayer time had consisted of the pastor praying with everyone else listening (or creating a shopping list, doodling on the bulletin, drifting off to sleep, etc.). Strongly convinced that the Lord wants everyone in His Body to know how to pray out loud with authority—and in corporate settings, not just in "prayer closets"—I felt that God was calling us to *be* the Kingdom in prayer. I also felt that a church is the safest place in the world to discover the power of praying for and with each other. Consequently, we provided time in the worship service when the congregation was asked to gather in groups of three to five people and pray out loud for one another.

The initial reaction to this change made the one about worship music seem mild. Although the congregation has been experiencing significant renewal in the Holy Spirit, many of them strongly resisted being asked to actually pray with and for each other publicly. In times like this, I appreciate the fact that, in my denominational system, a pastor cannot be fired. On the other hand, getting fired might have felt better than some of the comments, unsigned letters, and "disappearing saints" I had to endure (and grieve over).

Despite all the heartache at the time, the long-term Kingdom impact has been wonderful to watch. Although there is still some resistance to the prayer circles (let's face it, our flesh will always resist prayer!), there have been some profound breakthroughs. People are experiencing the Kingdom of God literally as Heaven flows through their hands and into their neighbors. The meaning of "the Kingdom of God is at hand" has become quite real to many folks.

I love the transformations that are taking place. For example, a woman in the congregation recently shared with me that her husband, who strongly disliked prayer circles initially, and who had previously never taken the lead in terms of prayer or ministry, has come to a radical and amazing new place. During a meeting at a local public school that the husband and wife had with an administrator (who in the course of the meeting had shared about a family crisis), this husband suggested that they pray. Taking the official's hands, he led him and his delighted but shocked wife in a much-appreciated and well-received time of prayer. This woman's account blessed my heart because I know that until men and women discover how to pray with one another in the safety of their churches, they'll never be able fully to administer Kingdom authority in the world!

Ignorance of Kingdom Dynamics Doesn't Change Them!

Whether we know it or not, Kingdom principles are always at work in and around and through us. For instance, every believer is constantly binding and loosing; we can't turn it on or off. Unfortunately, because we tend to believe the Kingdom operates by our choice rather than the King's dominion, we often are binding things that should be loosed, and loosing things that should be bound. Yes, we humans want to control when we're doing Kingdom stuff as well as when we're doing "our own thing." That kind of thinking is as ridiculous as thinking we can "turn off" the great confession of who Jesus is or His divine conception of who we are in Him!

Although those keys Jesus gave us may dangle unused for a long time, that doesn't negate the fact that He gave them to us! The Kingdom of God operates by His rules and in His perfect authority. The Kingdom of God reflects His being, character, and nature. The kingdom of satan, of course, operates in accordance with the devil's being, nature, and character. It is the realm of control, the kingdom of manipulation, domination, and intimidation. What a confused mess, then, when believers, armed with heavenly Kingdom authority, still choose to operate by satan's rules! Ultimately, we cannot live in two kingdoms. The discomfort that many of us church folks feel is the dichotomy of trying to do just that. James calls this dichotomy being *"double-minded,"* and reminds us that it makes one *"unstable in all his ways"* (James 1:8).

Peter found this out in a hurry! Having tried to control by manipulating the actions of King Jesus, Peter soon heard the words, *"Get behind Me, Satan!"* (Matt. 16:23). It is a painful lesson we all must learn. We cannot control God, there is nothing of control in or over Him, and Kingdom people should never default to that kind of fallen-kingdom behavior. We all do default on occasion, but the sooner we discover abundant life in the awesome authority of the Kingdom of God, the sooner we lay down the tools and behaviors of the kingdom of control.

The Kingdom—Now and Not Yet

Now let me tie this all together. The Kingdom of God is, of course, both "now" and "not yet." We should never forget that the "now" is a reflection of the "not yet" that is about to be—perfection restored, the Kingdom consummated. Until we recognize and set our hearts on the "not yet" reality of the Kingdom (the perfection that is coming), we cannot fully possess the "now" reality of the Kingdom, perfection in the making. To *be* the Kingdom now is greatly strengthened if we know what the end result will be. To set our course by the perfection that is coming helps to bring about perfection in the here and now. To set our sights on the Kingdom *to come* helps us recognize and operate fully in the Kingdom *that is*.

We have been commissioned to release Heaven wherever we go, but it surely helps to know what the real Heaven looks like. In the battle against the "gates of hell," it helps to know that, not only will those gates (satan's power) not prevail in the here and now, but also that they will not exist at all as a force against us. As Kingdom people in the here and now, let's "go on to perfection," "release Heaven" "bind the enemy," "loose" God's mercy and love, and use the "keys"—encouraged and confident in the Perfection-restored Kingdom which is "not yet," but is mighty soon! Let's *be* the Kingdom of Heaven, never reducing the Gospel to "going to Heaven." And let's not try to live in the Kingdom of God while still operating in the power of satan's kingdom.

From One to Two to Three to Two as One

In the beginning, there was but one Kingdom, the Kingdom of God. Of course saying "beginning" is just for our sake: Actually, the Kingdom of God is without beginning or end. At some point, in indescribable love, God created a second kingdom, the kingdom of man. He did this knowing perfectly well what it would cost: Christ is, after all, *"the Lamb slain from the foundation of the world"* (Rev. 13:8). This kingdom, in original perfection, was flawlessly aligned with the Kingdom of God. The kingdom of man, truly a *kingdom* by God's design, with dominion and authority and free will, was so perfectly aligned with God's Kingdom as to be virtually indistinguishable, although man's dominion and kingdom were limited to the physical realm around him. It was a perfect fit of course, as man's dominion in the physical realm flowed flawlessly from and under God's dominion over every realm.

Sadly, a third kingdom arose, not by God's design, but by lucifer's hateful rebellion. God had entrusted His angel lucifer with significant, though limited, spiritual authority and dominion. Lucifer took this gift of love and turned it inward, appointing himself king over a kingdom of control-hungry former angels. This kingdom, with rebellion as its foundation, deception as its currency, and control as its method of conquest, rose up in utter opposition to the Kingdom of God, *and* the kingdom of man in its original perfection.

With only limited authority and dominion in the spiritual realm and with free will gone astray, satan looked for an opportunity to extend his rule and solidify his diseased kingdom. Although overthrowing God was out of the question, a tantalizing prospect gripped satan: using his weapons of control to pull humanity's kingdom away from God and His Kingdom, and into the sway of his own.

The kingdom of man, with dominion limited to the earthly physical realm, is dependent upon a spiritual authority. As humanity handed over their dominion of the world to satan, the kingdom of man came out from direct submission to God and became a vassal state of the kingdom of hell. All of creation fell, and now groans for the day of redemption! (See Romans 8:20-23.)

Satan, however, miscalculated the length and depth of God's love! He had no idea how far God would go (and come!) to redeem humanity and restore perfection. While the kingdom of man continues to be bound to the hell Adam chose in original sin, we who are in Christ, the Second Adam, have a new spiritual covering. Furthermore, we are progressively moving toward the perfection He is restoring. We do so in the confidence that the gates of hell cannot prevail; that the current compromised position of the kingdom of man will soon give way to a perfect eternity in which the Kingdom of God will once again be the only spiritual sovereignty; and that the kingdom of man, once again in perfect submission, will rule and reign with Him forever and ever!

In the day perfection is restored, the kingdom of man will be perfectly aligned with the Kingdom of God and populated only by those who by free will chose God's Kingdom over satan's kingdom. In that day, there will once again be only two Kingdoms, but they will be perfectly and forever one.

As a song title says: "What a Day That Will Be"![1]

Perfection Restored

Revelation 22:1-5 gives us a most amazing glimpse into the totality of Christ's victory, the perfection once lost but now restored and soon realized. The passage reads:

And he showed me a pure river of water of life, clear as crystal, proceeding from the throne of God and of the Lamb. In the middle of its street, and on either side of the river, was the tree of life, which bore twelve fruits, each tree yielding its fruit every month. The leaves of the tree were for the healing of the nations. And there shall be no more curse, but the throne of God and of the Lamb shall be in it, and His servants shall serve Him. They shall see His face, and His name shall be on their foreheads. There shall be no night there: They need no lamp nor light of the sun, for the Lord God gives them light. And they shall reign forever and ever.

As the ancient hymn *Gloria Patra* declares: "As it was in the beginning, it is now [in the finished work of Jesus] and ever shall be [as that work is consummated] world without end [the new Heaven and earth, perfection restored], amen, amen!" In today's vernacular, what the hymn says (assuming that believers have a Kingdom foundation) is that, because the work of Jesus is already complete, we can now sing with absolute expectation of that perfect Kingdom to come. We are living in the Kingdom now, going on to perfection as if it already is!

Six Areas of Perfection

Look with me at six areas of perfection restored, along with the corresponding demise of control.

Perfect *life* restored (control's deadness gone) (Rev. 22:1): The *"pure river of water of life"* reminds us that life will be, as it was in the beginning, perfectly and completely in God. Life will be absolute, perfect *life!* No death, no disease, no destruction, no decline, just life, and that to the fullest! But what of control? Its "deadness" will be gone forever. Everything manifest in the attempt to be *god* apart from God was death. Eat its fruit, and you will *"surely die"* (Gen. 2:17)—and we did. But all the ravages of control and the death it brought will be gone in restored perfection!

Perfect *provision* restored (control's poverty gone) (see Rev. 22:2a): The Tree of Life, *Jesus,* was and is and forever will be the source of perfect provision. While we could not access the "fruit" of this tree in a fallen state, we should now be eating and actually producing fruit as we live now in the truth of the restoration. Everything we have ever needed is in Jesus, and in fact *is* Jesus. With the lust for control via manipulation, domination, and intimidation gone, the poverty in which it imprisons us will also be gone.

Perfect *unity* restored (control's divisions gone) (Rev. 22:2b): Those *"leaves...*[which are] *for the healing of the nations"* are a beautiful opposite of the fig leaves of control! Whereas control's leaves have brought nothing but division, war, conflict, blame, hate, and chaos, the Lord's leaves heal to perfect unity! We should be aware of a very important point here: the way we live together in the Church *now* absolutely reveals which leaves we're dressed in. There is no excuse for true believers to be anything other than instruments of God's relational healing!

Perfect *relationship* restored (The control-ite character gone) (see Rev. 22:3-4): With "no more curse" to bind, blind, and cripple us, all the damage of the Fall will be gone. We will be perfectly in the midst of God, in perfect service, in perfect dance, face to Face, with His name—His very nature and being—emblazoned upon us! We will live in faultless relationship with God, with the other saints, and within ourselves. What a vision of what our lives, awash in the grace of God, should be now!

Perfect *revelation* restored (control's darkness gone) (see Rev. 22:5a): The "light" that is God not only overcomes physical darkness; it also overcomes all the darkness and misunderstanding of the ages. With perfect communication, communion, and community restored, all confusion will be gone! And isn't it an amazing truth that Jesus is already *"the light of the world"*? (John 8:12)! When you think about it, we really have no excuse for living as if He isn't!

Perfect *dominion* restored (control forever gone!) (see Rev. 22:5b): To reign with God will mean that all vestiges of attempting to *be god* will forever be gone. With true authority and dominion restored, we will be seated again to reign! But isn't it a marvelous truth that we already *"sit together in the heavenly places in Christ Jesus"*? (Eph. 2:6) Perhaps, we should live *now* as if already in perfection!

As Dr. Robert Tuttle has said, "Too many of us simply don't know what we're missing because we do not realize what we had."[2] Let me add to that, "Too many of us don't know what we can become *now, by grace,* because we don't know what will soon be. The Kingdom of God is real, it has come, and it is here. A life truly lived in the Kingdom is a life lived apart from domination, intimidation, or manipulation. Once and for all, we must decide that we are not the *king!* And, once for all, we must trust the reality of grace, right here and now, to perfect us as Kingdom citizens, now and forever. The truth is that if we're not going on to perfection now, how do we think we will go to it *someday?* Is the power of the Holy Spirit really that limited? Is the effectiveness of the cross really that small? Are we truly trapped in the world, only to taste of the Kingdom after we die? Of course not! Our God is not small! He has already won the victory, His Kingdom is already here, and we are truly His people. By grace, we must go on to perfection, even and especially *now!*

Chapter Twelve

THE HEART OF CONTROL

It has been established that, in the Fall, we humans have inherited the nature of satan. We are born with *a heart of control,* and no amount of heart surgeries can repair *that* heart. Without the transplant of Jesus' heart, we will die in sin. God used the terminal illness of a beloved friend to bring me to a place of life in Christ Jesus, to a place where my heart of control gave way to the *heart of Jesus.*

Although I was six years older than Davy, he towered over me in terms of a deeply Spirit-filled relationship with the Lord. Born with cystic fibrosis, he was the bravest person I'd ever met (also among the most devout in Christian faith). Throughout his adolescent years, he valiantly fought his illness. However, when he was 18, a second disease, leukemia, began to attack his already weakened body. The doctors and nurses did everything they could for Davy, but the truth is that they were able only to treat the symptoms. They had no power over the source of the symptoms: they could not prevent the choking production of mucus in his body, nor could they inhibit the ravages of the cancer in his blood.

While praying for Davy's healing one night at a healing service, I suddenly had a revelatory moment much like Peter's when he made that famous declaration: *"You are the Christ, the Son of the living God"* (Matt. 16:16). I'd gone to church my whole life, but, for the first time in my life, I really *knew* that Jesus is God, that He is alive, and that He loves even me. I suddenly knew, and knew that I knew, that Jesus is the Christ. Later that evening, I experienced the baptism with the Holy Spirit. In my brokenness, God had been able both to reveal and seal His redemption of my life. What an amazing healing!

A couple of weeks later, death snatched Davy away from his failed physical tent, but Jesus snatched him away from death! Davy's death, of course, was devastating to all who knew him; however, the "sting of death" was assuaged in light of the healing that I (and many others) experienced in the midst of his dying. Furthermore, revelatory moments kept coming to me.

I began realizing spiritual truths about things that had transpired in the illness and death of my friend. Doctors and nurses could not treat the source of Davy's illness (the *heart* of his symptoms); yet, flowing from his true heart (from his very nature and being) was a healing stream that impacted many lives, reflecting the fact that Davy was truly a transformed, Spirit-filled, light-shining, Jesus-loving saint of God. Because he looked, loved, and lived remarkably like the Lord, it was clear that somehow in the course of his short life, he'd had a *heart transplant.*

Matthew 15:10-20 is an extraordinary passage dealing with some important contrasts: (1) the difference between outward acts, religion, and inward transformation, life in Christ Jesus, (2) the difference between a symptom, like control, and the source of the symptom— our very nature, (3) and the difference between a Band-Aid (a work of the flesh), and the cure (a new heart). Simply said, we need our controlling heart removed and the heart of Jesus implanted! It's not enough to make superficial changes by an act of our will in an effort to reduce our "symptoms." It's not enough to bandage the problem. It's not enough to be "better"; we need to be healed to the core; we need a new heart!

> *When He had called the multitude to Himself, He said to them, "Hear and understand: Not what goes into the mouth defiles a man; but what comes out of the mouth, this defiles a man." Then His disciples came and said to Him, "Do You know that the Pharisees were offended when they heard this saying?"*

But He answered and said, "Every plant which My heavenly Father has not planted will be uprooted. Let them alone. They are blind leaders of the blind. And if the blind leads the blind, both will fall into a ditch." Then Peter answered and said to Him, "Explain this parable to us." So Jesus said, "Are you also still without understanding? Do you not yet understand that whatever enters the mouth goes into the stomach and is eliminated? But those things which proceed out of the mouth come from the heart, and they defile a man. For out of the heart proceed evil thoughts, murders, adulteries, fornications, thefts, false witness, blasphemies. These are the things which defile a man, but to eat with unwashed hands does not defile a man" (Matthew 15:10-20).

Our human desire and capacity to intimidate, manipulate, or dominate others emanates from our heart, our very being, not from bad teaching or inadequate nurture. Control is the symptom; a corrupted, fallen nature is the source. Treating the symptoms may make us temporarily somewhat better; but our only real hope is for our hearts to be radically and permanently cured. Psychology may offer some Band-Aids, but Jesus offers us a cure—a new heart, a new nature, a new *ontology!* Our "heart of control" must be removed, and the heart of Jesus implanted! Otherwise, we are just washing our hands, while spewing out satanic garbage. We're just pretending to be whole based on outward acts, while our hearts remain hopelessly sick. The good news, of course, is that Jesus has come to change our *hearts,* not just bandage our actions.

We have looked at the *Game of Control,* which all humans, by our very nature, play. We have recognized the *Source of Control,* which is, in a word, satan. We have acknowledged the *Breadth of Control,* which is from Genesis to Revelation, including every human being since Adam's fall except Jesus, who knew no control. We have looked at the *Opposite of Control,* which is God the Father, Son, and Holy Spirit's very nature and character. We have seen that *Overcoming Control* is made possible by true maturity in the Lord and holiness by the Lord. We have documented the *End of Control* as perfection is restored, challenging one another to live in this Kingdom reality now. Finally, we have noted that the true cure for us involves being changed to the core as the *Heart of Control* gives way to the heart of Jesus.

What fruit will be evident? *Mutual submission* as the very framework of relationship will certainly be one fruit. Lives free from control are submitted lives, in which love for one another replaces the desire to lord over one another.

Servant ministry will also be evident as the desire to control gives way to a passion to serve. This requires an inner security that only a deep relationship with Jesus brings. Insecure people control out of their very insecurity.

A *daily relationship* with God—a dancing one at that—will certainly manifest in our human spirits, even as an ongoing *dying to self* will proceed in our souls. As our relationship with the Almighty deepens, our "need" to be God decreases.

A *soul*-based desire, fueled by a grace-ladened *spirit*, will propel us *toward perfection* in the here and now. With control gone, we can and must love God with all of our heart, soul, mind, and strength.

Our *spirit*, full of God's grace, and "dripping wet" with repentance, intimacy, and power, will lead our *soul* onward, and prepare us for a new *body*. With victory assured, perfection in sight, and the King reigning over His Kingdom, the reality of living as a restored human trinity reflecting the glory of the Triune God is not only possible, but it is the only goal worth having.

Perfection, or "going on to perfection," begins with the heart. Thus, it behooves us to examine what is proceeding out of our own hearts. What deep-to-the-core transformation and regeneration needs to take place in our hearts in order to walk in true Christianity, as opposed to "Control-ianity"? Is it really possible to be control-free? Well, of course it is, since it is all by grace. And since it is all by grace, and grace is freely given, the compelling question for you and me is: *Why not now?*

Chapter Thirteen

PROFILES IN CHARACTER

Long before John F. Kennedy wrote *Profiles in Courage,* the Almighty God wrote a book that, in the context of this project, might best be entitled *Profiles in Character.* The book of Job gives powerful insights into the ontological makeup of God and satan, as well as intriguing glimpses into the ontological composition of humanity. Three of Job's "friends" picture for us the manifestation of the control tendencies of domination, manipulation, and intimidation; a fourth friend gives us a glimpse of how the Holy Spirit woos us back toward God. Job himself is an intriguing shadow and type of the *Suffering Servant.* It seems fitting to close out this book with a quick perusal of the Book of Job.

It should come as no surprise that God's sovereignty, power, wisdom, and mercy all come through clearly in this book. As Charles Blair shares:

> The Book of Job teaches several lessons: 1) God is sovereign. We cannot understand His workings by rational thinking alone; faith must rest in God's love and our knowledge of Him. Sovereignty means that God is all-powerful; He knows all, He is everywhere present, and His decision is final (see Jer. 4:8; Dan. 4:17). God is the author of all the power of the universe. 2) We understand ourselves and our

lives in direct relationship to our understanding that God's will toward us is good (see John 10:10), that God cares and communicates His caring to his children—as He did to Job—this changes everything. Faith must have a resting place. When deep suffering threatens the foundations of faith, as was the case with Job, an assault on our faith can destroy us unless we are firmly rooted in these truths.[1]

Not only do all the realities of God's ontology, of which Blair speaks, become evident as one reads the text of Job, but also a key insight into the attitude necessary for one to come to greater knowledge of, and deeper intimacy with, the Lord. Humility is not optional. The perfect Humility that is God must be approached in humility, particularly if one desires to walk in relationship with Him. He may come like a whirlwind (see Job 38:1-41), but the goal is for persons to humbly approach Him. When people do, the ontological reality of God is impossible to hide. In other words, it is not possible to conceal His kindness and integrity. God speaks, strengthens, encourages, and as necessary, corrects, so that humans can find themselves fully in Him.[2]

Not only is God's ontology profiled in the Book of Job, but so also is satan's, beginning with his name. *Satan* means "opponent," "the hater," "the accuser," "adversary or enemy," and one who resists or hinders all that is good.[3] Satan is neither omnipresent nor omniscient, he lacks the ability to act without divine permission, and even then, his power and scope are always limited.[4] Apparently, satan is so trapped in his own ontological darkness as to be blind to the reality that God allows his attacks and siftings to assail humanity only in order to perfect (sanctify) humanity. Ironically, satan's desire to destroy humanity is useful at times to God in His passion to rescue humanity! Satan is no more than a pawn in the things of God which are obviously far too grand and majestic for satan to comprehend. The devil's smallness of character is dramatically contrasted to God's greatness in the Book of Job. Although it appears for a while that Job is the pawn in this drama, the fact is that satan is really the pawn. God is never fooled or deceived, and His people are always the better for it.

Of particular interest, however, is the ontological picture presented through Job's three friends Eliphaz, Bildad, and Zophar, as well as the very different and later encounter with a fourth friend, Elihu. I contend that the first three represent the control trinity of domination, manipulation, and intimidation; the fourth, it seems, is something of a picture of the Holy Spirit's efforts to help humans humbly seek the Lord. While none of Job's friends were completely wrong, none were completely right—especially the first three. Like Job, they were all ignorant of satan's attacks, and it was evident. Still, their incomplete theological understandings were further twisted and contorted by their efforts to control Job, the situation, and their own pain (and fear) over Job's condition. Blame, as old as The Garden, is a prime tool of control. If Job's problems were his own fault, then Eliphaz, Bildad, and Zophar could control their own situations—by not being like Job. There is a certain arrogant bliss in ignorance and judgment.

Eliphaz the Manipulator

Eliphaz has been called the "most sympathetic of the com-forters."[5] His rather kind and apologetic words in the first several verses of his opening dialogue, recorded in chapter four, belie the fact that he strongly felt that Job had brought his suffering upon himself. The point of interest here, however, is his technique to impart this "truth." By attempting to bring a hard message of blame in a gentle and roundabout way, Eliphaz was operating in manipulation. Using proverbs, parables, hymns, and even a claim to revelation from a vision,[6] Eliphaz attempted to make his point.

To this author and, no doubt, many others who are active in the charismatic/Pentecostal stream of the Church, the use of personal prophecies or revelations to manipulate people and situations is painfully familiar. Not that this reality should make the Church despise prophecies, as is made clear in First Thessalonians 5:20, but the reality is that "prophetic control" is an all-too real occurrence which can quench the Spirit (see 1 Thess. 5:19), and must be tested as to true motivation (see 1 Thess. 5:21). As is almost always the case, Eliphaz's great revelation proved only to be a common truism, rather than a profound word from God.[7] But as a tool of control, claiming divine authority can be quite effective.

Eliphaz's manipulation was an attempt to get Job to confess guilt. Not only would this have made Eliphaz feel wise in his comprehension of the situation, but it would have made him feel more secure in the sense that such devastation could not befall him. Control is often not only about self-promotion and position, but also about self-vindication and justification. Eliphaz may have been more gentle than the other two "friends" at this juncture in the Book, but his attempts to control Job and thus control his own situation were no less misguided than theirs.

Bildad the Dominator

Bildad's approach to Job was not as gentle as Eliphaz's. Blatantly and abrasively accusing Job of being windbag,[8] Bildad, in the language of this project, obviously was a dominator. Rather than claim and rely on prophetic revelation as a platform to confront, as Eliphaz did, Bildad claimed tradition as his authority.[9]

Using tradition as a weapon of domination within a church setting is all too familiar to most pastors, particularly those who, like this author, serve in mainline movements and in long-established congregations. Tradition provides a strong and dominating position upon which control can often be gained. As Elmer Smick shares concerning Bildad:

> Bildad's speech contains an important negative lesson about human nature in general and about the qualities of a good counselor. He heard Job's words with his ears, but his heart heard nothing. This truth should be viewed in the light of Job's plea for compassion in chapter 6. All people under the most ordinary circumstances need compassion; how much more Job in his extremity![10]

This hearing with ears but not with the heart can often happen when everything entering the ears (and heart) is filtered through the lens of tradition, with a desire to control in operation. Bildad, like Eliphaz before him, desired to control the situation, to make Job's hurt go away, and to make sense in a way that would guarantee that Bildad wouldn't find himself in Job's shoes. Bildad, however, operated in domination rather than manipulation, but there is another key point to make at this juncture.

Bildad's speech, as was the case with Eliphaz and Zophar, did contain elements of truth. One of the key ontological points taught in the book of Job is that truth and control are not mutually exclusive. Many prophecies are legitimate words from God, and tradition can be a rich and powerful anchor. But once manipulation or domination (or intimidation) enters the situation, the authority and truthfulness of the foundation of the prophecy is perverted by the intent to control. Control-ism misuses truth so as to devalue it; its ultimate goal isn't Truth (as in an ontological reality of the Godhead) but rather control (as in an attempt to play God).

Zophar the Intimidator

Concerning the third "friend" mentioned in Job, Carl Shultz says, "Zophar lacks the courtesy of Eliphaz. He seems to be totally devoid of sympathy. His dogmatism is apparent when he claims that Job cannot possibly know the unsearchable wisdom of God."[11] Zophar does not hesitate to make Job the adversary in this discussion, and to lunge directly for his jugular. In the language of this project, the desire for confrontation with a dogged determination to be correct at all costs is called *intimidation*. That dogmatism, a certainty of being right, motivated Zophar to intimidate should come as no surprise. That a portion of Zophar's reasoning was simplistic, or that elements of his theology misguided, should also not be surprising.[12] What this author hopes *is* surprising, or at least interesting to readers, is the fact that these three friends so explicitly illustrate the three forms of control outlined in this project.

While Job's friends demonstrate that individuals operate primarily out of their predominant control trait, Job's response is a study in how people, when pressed, can experience feelings of domination, intimidation, and manipulation. Job's reactions range from being angry and confrontational (see Job 13:1-12; 16:2-19), to being remorseful (see Job 19:21), to feeling hurt and injured (see Job 19:3). His responses, however, emanate from the same basic source as that of his friends, human nature bent on controlling self, life, and others, until a fourth friend confronts him in a different manner, and God Himself enters the discussion.

Elihu—A Picture of the Holy Spirit

Elihu, the fourth friend in the book of Job, is different from the other three for a key reason: Elihu, while by no means perfect, was nevertheless attempting to speak truth into the situation while at the same time not exhibiting a controlling nature. Elihu was angry at Job's three friends and at Job himself.[13] Yet his approach was the most gentle of all; and, while angry with Job for his self-righteousness, Elihu nonetheless was attempting to aid Job, not by endeavoring to explain the situation or to cast blame but by encouraging humility before God. In doing so, Elihu was evincing the work of the Holy Spirit. As Charles Blair states:

> Elihu, in his debate with Job, makes three significant statements about the role of the Holy Spirit in the relationship of people to God. In 32:8 he declares that a person's understanding is not due to his age or station in life, but rather is a result of the operation of the Spirit of God. The Spirit then is the Author of wisdom, endowing one with the capacity to know and making sense out of life for him. Thus knowledge and wisdom are the Spirit's gift to men.
>
> The Spirit is also the Source of life itself (33:4). Apart from the direct influence of the Spirit, man as we know him would not have come into existence. From the original Creation it was so, and continues to be so. The Spirit of God is the Spirit of life.

Because the Spirit gives life and wisdom to man, He is also essential to the very continuation of the human race. If God should turn His attention elsewhere, if He should withdraw His life-giving Spirit from this world, then human history would come to an end (34:14,15). Elihu's point is that God is neither capricious nor selfish.[14]

The fact that God chose to expose such attributes concerning the Person of the Spirit through Elihu is indicative of Elihu's role in this Book, that of modeling the work of the Spirit. The difference between Elihu and the others wasn't simply his age; it was his basic motivation. Elihu concluded his remarks with the call to fear God, because *"He shows no partiality to any who are wise of heart"* (Job 37:24). In the language of this project, He shows no partiality to any who control or to any form of control.

Job—A Picture of Jesus the Suffering Servant

We are all aware that Moses is a type or picture of Jesus, not a perfect picture, of course, but a powerful one nonetheless. Moses helps us understand Jesus as *Mediator*. David, too, is clearly seen as a type of Christ. He pictures well (but not perfectly) Jesus' role as *Priest* and *King*.

Job, too, is a type of Jesus, particularly in His full humanity as the *Suffering Servant*. Sure, there are some striking differences. Job was unaware of satan's attacks, while Jesus was fully aware of them. Job's exposure to the raw hate of satan was tempered; Jesus experienced the fullness of satan's rage. Still, notice the striking similarities between Job's cries in Job 17, and Jesus' in Psalm 22. Job serves to picture for us Jesus as He suffered outrageously at the hands of control-freak humans and ultimately satan himself. While Jesus' reaction to the obscene injustice of His suffering was marked by perfection throughout, unlike Job's, the startling value of Job's suffering as a picture pointing to Christ's suffering is still amazing to see. Just as Job humbly submitted himself to God's righteousness, Jesus, burdened with the sin of the world, submitted perfectly to His Father's righteous judgment. He was obedient even unto death, and He was exalted to the highest place (see Phil. 2:8-9).

Just as Job suffered the loss of his first family, Jesus lost His beloved children to the Fall. Job eventually enjoyed a new, and much more grateful, family. Jesus, too, is enjoying a family of redeemed children who display a gratitude born of knowing what they were redeemed out of. Job ended up better at the end than he was at the beginning. Jesus, too, will enjoy perfection with those who have chosen perfection (Him), versus those who were born into it as were Adam and Eve. This family (all of us) will be forever grateful to the One who suffered so violently to give us the chance to live and reign with Him forever and ever.

Jesus had to put up with some misguided friends and their manipulations, dominations, and intimidations. He had to put up with many enemies who used the same tactics ultimately to crucify Him. Furthermore, Jesus had to put up with the ultimate intimidator, dominator, and manipulator of them all: fallen lucifer. But Jesus did so perfectly, with the loving help of the Holy Spirit, who stood alongside Jesus as He kept His focus on the Beloved Father and His will.

A Better Way to Read the Book of Job

The Book of Job, then, is an amazing presentation of *Profiles in Character.* Not only does viewing the work from this perspective make the book of special interest to this project, it also makes the Book of Job more valuable to the Church in general. The Book of Job deals, not only with humanity's attempts to understand and deal with human pain, but also, and more importantly, with the ontological distinctions between God and satan and with the fallen manifestations of human ontology (twisted by the Fall into the image of satan) as they try to be "God" to each other. Only the Holy Spirit can guide us to God, and humility on our part is the only (but absolutely necessary) requirement. Jesus embodied perfect humility that, in the face of the ultimate suffering, never ever lost sight of the perfect will of the Father.

Ontologically, control simply is not embodied in God; nor is it respected by God. Even though Job's first three friends expressed certain elements of theological truth, the only counsel Job really required was the necessity for him to humbly submit to God. Answers are not what one needs from God; God Himself is what we desperately need from God! Humility, then, is a powerful antidote to the human tendency to control.

The True Friends of Jesus

We need to ask ourselves whether we are true friends of Jesus. Or are we more like Job's friends? They intimidated, manipulated, and dominated in a very fallen attempt to lay blame and to control their own circumstances. Their *friendship* revolved around their own wants, desires, and *needs*. And the same with Jesus' friends and family before their redemption! After all, they were just fallen humans in need of a Savior. After the resurrection and Pentecost, these same friends became *true friends*.

Jesus Himself illustrated the standard of true friendship:

> *Greater love has no one than this, than to lay down one's life for his friends. You are My friends if you do whatever I command you* (John 15:13-14).

Truly, Jesus laid down His life for us; and we are His true friends only as we lay down control and replace it with obedience (John 15:14-15). His friendship releases grace, supernatural power, enabling us to do whatever He commands us, free from the junk that once controlled us. The true friends of Jesus deeply love one another (vs. 12) and intimately know their Master (vs.15). If we do not measure up to the standard Jesus exemplified, we need to repent of everything in us that behaves like one of Job's friends. We need to receive the extraordinary grace of God and be transformed. Only in laying down our lives, especially the hell-bent desire to control, can we be friends— Jesus' friends! Jesus' friend! My prayer for all of us who call ourselves "Christian" is that our *Game of Control* will end as the joy of being a true friend of God blossoms in each of us.

Epilogue

Help! I'm Losing Control!

Yes, I am losing control; however, my cry for help is for aid in the continued effort to lay down every vestige of the Game of Control. By the grace of God, much has changed in my life since that long drive to Indiana almost a decade ago, but I'm still "going on to perfection." I want to dance that *Divine Dance!*

As I have become more aware of control in my own life, I have prayed, fasted, repented, and generally sought the Lord for the transformation in my soul needed to cease playing the game. While I certainly don't profess perfection (yet) in the process, I can certainly see progress over the years. I am much less prone to manipulate situations than I used to be. The whole process of control has become much clearer and more disgusting to me.

Truthfully, being significantly set free from control-ism has greatly simplified my life as a husband, father, and pastor. I don't waste near as much time trying to get my way via control. I have been greatly blessed in this because my wife, recognizing her own control nature (domination), has also experienced significant healing. God in His love is doing a great work in both of us.

I have also become much more sensitive to people's attempts to get their way with me by using domination, intimidation, or manipulation. By God's grace, I don't waste much time judging or correcting them for it. (Of course any judging on my part is wrong, and correcting really needs to come from the Lord, not me.) I just recognize it for what it is and go on, deeply aware of my own frailty of soul.

Before I end the book, I feel the need to briefly share two things. First, I struggled a great deal, especially early on, with how to deal with stuff and people apart from manipulation. It had been such an integral part of who I was that, at times, I didn't quite know how to behave without it. It just came so *naturally*. But, through repeated recognition, repentance, and prayer, the urge to control through manipulation receded greatly. This soul-transformation business takes time, even if one is so full of Father, Son, and Holy Spirit in your spirit as to "drip" constantly!

Secondly, I think I need to say that people sometimes didn't (and still don't) quite know what to make of me. Control, politics, and game playing are so much a part of "normal" life—even in the Church—that beginning to not play along can drive some folks insane. It can make some people downright angry, especially if they are quite good at manipulating, intimidating, or dominating. When controlling diminishes in one's life, the power of being controlled also diminishes. This fact can really perturb some folks, even (or especially!) if they are told what God is doing!

Hopefully, sharing these thoughts will encourage my readers. It takes time and patience to heal. Love and grace will have to be extended to those who, still trapped in the game, will offer some pretty strange opposition. Although we were all born slaves to the warped and vain imaginations of our satan-savaged souls, we can, by the grace of God, be born again and filled up with such power that we, over time, can quit playing God. May this be our prayer and an ever-increasing reality in our churches, families, and friends! To God alone be the glory, Amen.

Appendix

THE ROCK/PAPER/SCISSORS CURRICULUM

Overview:

The Rock/Paper/Scissors (RPS) Curriculum was developed to help identify and address the control-game-playing tendencies found in all human beings and to discover in Jesus the way to live life essentially free from the game. Controlling and being controlled is the familiar game (cycle) of life which dates all the way back to the Fall of humanity, when the basic nature of humankind was distorted to look more like the nature of satan than the nature (being) of God. Since the Fall, humans have been trying to "get their way" with each other in a seemingly unending game of manipulation, domination, and intimidation, a sort of behavioral "unholy trinity" as opposed to the Love, Humility, and Truth which describe the very being of the Holy Trinity. This curriculum compares domination, intimidation, and manipulation with the familiar game of Rock/Paper/Scissors to illustrate both the nature of the game, and the ultimate goal of overcoming it, through the grace of our Lord Jesus Christ.

This curriculum is designed to be used only in a setting saturated with the grace of the Lord Jesus, the love of the Father, and the communion of the Holy Spirit. Otherwise, the teaching contained in this material can actually enhance and encourage the very thing the Lord desires to transform out of us all, control-ism!

This curriculum has been prepared so that it can be used in a variety of settings, including retreats, Sunday School settings, or a multipart sermon series. But before teaching RPS, spend significant time in prayer, repentance, and reflection before the Lord. Control is so deeply rooted in all of us as to become our very nature apart from the sanctifying work of Father, Son, and Holy Spirit. Using any part of this teaching as a weapon against another defeats the purpose entirely and exposes heart motives in ourselves that are in need of healing and deliverance. But when taught (and received) in a Spirit-filled, humble, and submitted place, this course has, in Jesus, the power to set people free!

It is my prayer that freedom and healing, mutual submission and servant-ministry, agape love and reclamation of true dominion will break forth in your ministry and those you've been called to serve as you use this material—to the glory of the glorious name of our Triune God!

Your brother by the blood,
Craig A. Green

Course Purposes

This seminar seeks to assist participants to:
1. discover human control tendencies, intimidation/manipulation/ domination;
2. identify their own dominant control technique;
3. recognize the futility and frustration associated with the game of control;
4. repent of "control-ism";
5. develop a deeper understanding of the biblical concept of mutual submission;
6. develop a deeper appreciation for, and participation in, "servant ministry";

7. appreciate the ontological makeup within the Holy Trinity;
8. recognize the ontological makeup of satan, and its transfer to humanity in the Fall;
9. discover the theme of control as presented throughout the Bible;
10. recognize the scriptural mandate to identify and repent of control traits;
11. appreciate the Church's calling to help conquer control-ite tendencies;
12. celebrate the transformational power of God to move believers from control-ism to restored dominion.

Learning Outcomes

Upon satisfactory completion of this seminar, participants will have:

1. confronted the depths of fallen human nature in the area of controlling/being controlled;
2. developed a clear differentiation between relational theology, as pictured in the Godhead and lived out in the Church through mutual submission, and a selfish "*me*-ology" based on satan's rebellion, and lived out in unredeemed humanity;
3. analyzed the various forms of control at work in humanity and their origin;
4. heard clearly the Lord's disgust with control-ism, and His call to repent;
5. visualized the difference between "control" and "dominion";
6. recognized the Church's responsibility to confront the sin of control-ism of every type and on every level;
7. developed a plan of action to lay down control, and to actively pursue mutual submission;
8. acquired an appreciation for "original righteousness," and the resulting gift of dominion, and the biblical tools to be restored to it by grace.

Outline:

Lesson One—*The Game of Control* (Eph. 4:11-16)

1. My Story (Feb. 2000)—"My war with the church treasurer" (Or an appropriate personal story of *control* by the instructor)
2. The Game of R/P/S—Domination/Manipulation/Intimidation (Rock = domination; Paper = manipulation; Scissors = intimidation) A winless game, a vicious cycle
3. *"You will be like God"—all* humans by nature are "control freaks."
4. A help to *self*-identification—qualities most valued, and those least desired

CONTROL TYPE:	VALUE MOST:	HATE:
Dominators	Winning	Losing
Intimidators	Being right	Being embarrassed
Manipulators	Being accepted	Conflict/confrontation

It is important to note that permission is *never* given for people to start judging or identifying others. We are only responsible for our own behavior; we are *not* God, and cannot "fix" others (or ourselves for that matter, but we can repent, and allow God to turn us around!) It is important that participants be reminded of this.

1. Definitions of *domination, intimidation,* and *manipulation.* (Webster's)

   Domination: To dominate is "to rule or control; to exert the supreme determining or guiding influence on; to occupy the most prominent position in or over something."[1]

   Intimidation: To intimidate is "to make timid or fearful; to frighten; to discourage or suppress by threats or by violence."[2]

   Manipulation: To manipulate is "to handle or manage shrewdly and deviously for one's own profit."[3]

2. Servant ministry vs. being *"children tossed to and fro"*
3. Equipped to stop playing control games! (Why servant ministry isn't optional in the Kingdom!)

Lesson Two—*The Source of Control* (Gen. 1:26-28)

1. Dominion vs. control (love and sel*fless*ness vs. lust and sel*fish*ness)
2. God's being vs. satan's being (love, humility, and truth, vs. domination, intimidation, and manipulation)
3. God—3 in 1 (selfless relationship, perfect mutual submission)
4. The early Church fathers had a term *Perichoresis,* "Divine Dance"—"living *with, through,* and *in* each other," perfect relationship, love, humility, unity, and truth.

"God is not some faceless, all-powerful abstraction. God is Father, Son, and Holy Spirit, existing in a passionate and joyous fellowship. The Trinity is not three highly committed religious types sitting around in some room in heaven. The Trinity is a circle of shared life, and the life shared is full, not empty, abounding and rich and beautiful, not lonely and sad and boring."—Dr. C. Baxter Kruger[3]

"The Trinity is a true Trinity; not a numbering of unlike things, but a binding together of equals. Each of the Persons is God in the fullest sense. The Son and the Holy Ghost have their source of Being in the Father, but in such sense that they are fully consubstantial with Him, and that neither of Them differs from Him in any particular Essence."—Saint Gregory of Nazianzus, A.D. 329-389.[4]

1. The Creation and Garden—a picture of God's ontology (self-being), and humanity's original ontology.
2. Humans—3 in 1 (body, soul, and spirit)

Created to have Perichoresis with God...

Created to have Perichoresis within self...

These 3 together describe what the Lord's Supper pictures & prefigures.

Created to have Perichoresis with each other...

3. Satan—1 in 1. (spirit being) (selfish loner)—Mimics the Holy Trinity with the unholy trinity of intimidation, manipulation, domination.

4. Satan's own fall—The warping of his character (see Isa. 14:12-17; Ezek. 28:11-19)

Domination: *"By the abundance of your trading..."* (Ezek. 28:16).

Intimidation: *"Your heart was lifted up because of your beauty"* (Ezek. 28:17).

Manipulation: *"You corrupted your wisdom for the sake of your splendor..."* (Ezek. 28:17).

1. The Fall of humanity (see Gen. 3:1-7), satan's ontology (vv. 1-5) and the transfer of his ontology (vv 6-7) to humanity (see John 8:44-45).

2. Fig Leaves—dressed in the counterfeit of control.

3. Restoration in Christ Jesus to Original Righteousness.
Original Righteousness—(GOOD NEWS!)
Original Righteousness lost = Original Sin—(BAD NEWS!)
Original Righteousness—prone again, by Grace—(GOOD NEWS!)

"Too many of us simply don't know what we're missing because we do not know what we had."—Dr. Robert Tuttle[5]

Lesson Three—*The Breadth of Control* (Luke 4:1-13)

1. Control from Genesis to Revelation...
   A. Ezekiel 28:16-17—Satan's fall; wealth, splendor, and beauty corrupted.
   B. Genesis 3:1-5—The temptations in The Garden
   C. Genesis 3:6-7—The transfer of ontology (personality)
   D. Luke 4:1-13—The temptations of Christ
   E. Matthew 26:36-46—The final temptations of Christ

Control Type	Realm of Attack	Satan's Fall *Ezek.* 28:16-17	First Temptation *Gen. 3:1-5*	Transfer *Gen. 3:6-7*	Temptation of Christ *Luke 4:1-13*	Final Temptation *Matt. 26:36-46*	Works of Flesh *Gal. 5:16-24*	The World *1 John 2:16*	False Teachers *Jude 11*	In the Church *Rev. 2-3*	Final Battle *Rev. 16:13*
Domi-nation	Physical (Body)	Wealth—"filled with violence"	"You will not surely die"	"The tree was good for food"	"Command this stone to become bread"	"This cup"… …*Asleep*	"Selfish ambition"	"The lust of the flesh"	"The way of Cain"	"Doctrine of the Nicolaitans"	The beast (The antichrist)
Manip-ulation	Emotional (Soul)	Corrupt wisdom—"your splendor"	"Has God indeed said…?"	"It was pleasant to the eyes"	"The devil… showed Him all the kingdoms"	"This cup"… …*Asleep*	"Discord dissensions"	"The lust of the eyes"	"The error of Balaam"	"Doctrine of Balaam"	The dragon (satan)
Intimi-dation	Spiritual (Spirit)	Heart pride—"your beauty"	"You will be like God"	"A tree desirable to make one wise"	"Throw Yourself down from here"	"This cup"… …*Asleep*	"Fits of rage; outbursts of wrath"	"The pride of life"	"The rebellion of Korah"	"That woman Jezebel…a prophetess"	The false prophet

    F. Galatians 5:16-24—the works of the flesh, hate (as opposed to the fruit of the Spirit, love)

    G. First John 2:16—All that is of the world (evil sphere) is not of the Father.

    H. Jude 11—False teachers are so called because they D/M/I.

    I. Revelation 2-3

        1. "Nicolaitans" = domination of the Laos (Rev. 2:6,15);

        2. "Balaam" = manipulation (Num. 31:16);

        3. "Jezebel" = intimidation. (1 Kings 19:2)

    J. Revelation 16:13—Control manifested in the false trinity of the dragon, beast, and false prophet.

  2. Jesus resisted every temptation, giving us the hope of restoration, Jesus the Second Adam. (See Romans 5:14-15; First Corinthians 15:20-24, 45-48.)

Lesson Four—*The Opposite of Control* (Eph. 5:21)

1. *Love*, opposite of *domination* (Love is descriptive of the Father—see 1 John 4:8)

2. *Humility*, opposite of *intimidation* (Humility descriptive of Son—see Phil. 2:5-11)

3. *Truth*, opposite of *manipulation* (Truth descriptive of Holy Spirit—see John 16:13; 1 John 5:6)

4. "Submitting one to another"—love, humility and truth released in relationships.

5. *"I also am a man **under** authority"* (Matt. 8:9). Only when *under* authority do we *have* true authority. Dominion is being *under* authority. Control is an attempt to usurp authority, as modeled by satan. Control, then, is the attempt to *have* authority without being *under* it!

6. Servant Ministry (see Eph. 4:11-16)

7. Having the mind of Christ (see Phil. 2:5-11)

8. The hope of transformation: *"Therefore you shall be perfect..."* (Matt 5:48).

Control Type	Unredeemed Examples	Most Valued:	Key Scriptures	Changed by:	Redeemed by Grace:	New Value:	Perfected By:
Domination	Saul (*Jewish*)	Winning	Acts 9:1-30	Love	Paul (*Greek*)	Finishing	"Love your enemies" Matt 5:44
Manipulation	Simon *"Hear Me"*	Being Accepted	Matthew 16:13-23	Truth	Peter *"Little rock"*	Being Faithful	"Made perfect in one" John 17:23
Intimidation	James, *unbelieving half brother to Jesus in the flesh*	Being Right	John 7:3-4, I Cor. 15:7	Humility	James, *Apostle: Full brother to Jesus by the Spirit*	Being Godly	"A perfect man, able to bridle" James 3:2

The Way of Redemption by Grace:
1. Confession of control type
2. Repentance (the power of God meeting you and turning you around in your decision to forsake control-ism)
3. Reception of Love, Truth, Humility = TRANSFORMATION!

Lesson Five—*Overcoming Control* (Rev. 12:7-12)
1. *"The blood of the Lamb"*—Satan can't **manipulate** believers who know who and whose they are by and in the blood. (Victory over emotional attacks)
2. *Accepted* in the Beloved by the blood!
3. *And the compulsion to manipulate others fades away!*
4. *"The word of their testimony"*—Satan can't **intimidate** believers whose testimony is alive in the Word. (Victory over spiritual attacks)
5. *Right*—and willing to testify to it!
6. *And the compulsion to intimidate others fades away!*
7. *"They did not love their lives"*—Satan can't **dominate** those who have already given their lives away. (Victory over physical attacks)
8. *Winning*—by dying to self!
9. *And the compulsion to dominate others fades away!*
10. Note the difference between spiritual (overcoming) Christianity, and carnal Christianity (see 1 Cor. 2:12–3:4).

"Natural Man"—"Can't receive the things of God"
"Carnal Man"—"Babes in Christ" (saved, but still "natural" character)
"Spiritual Man"—"Has the mind of Christ"

OVERCOMING CHRISTIANS HAVE:
- A maturing, character-of-God type faith.
- Been baptized by Jesus with the Holy Spirit.
- Been crucified (in the Holy Spirit) to the flesh and its passions. (See Gal. 5:24; Rom. 8:13)
- A "going on to perfection," "meat not milk" relationship with God.

- The only Christians who overcome satan and his character are mature ones, Spirit-filled ones, blood-washed/testifying/crucified ones.
- Many Christians are still "babes" who cannot overcome satan!
- "Overcoming" Christianity is *normal* Christianity!

Summary: Willingly allow the Holy Spirit to administer the work of the cross to the rebellion of our flesh, a willingness to humbly repent, an attitude of mutual submission, a lifestyle of servant ministry, an overcomer's position, by the blood, the Word, and daily cross.

Lesson Six—*The End of Control—Perfection Restored* (Rev. 22:1-5)

1. **Perfect *life* restored** (control's deadness gone) (v. 1)
2. **Perfect *provision* restored** (control's poverty gone) (v. 2a)
3. **Perfect *unity* restored** (control's relational damage gone) (v. 2b)
4. **Perfect *relationship* restored** (The control-ite character gone) (vv. 3-4)
5. **Perfect *revelation* restored** (control's darkness gone) (v. 5a)
6. **Perfect *dominion* restored** (control forever and ever gone) (v. 5b)

Perfection: Once we've recognized what God desires for us, we have no alternative but to pursue it with passion in Holy Spirit power! (See Hebrews 6:1.) When? Now! Where? Here! How? By the grace of our Lord Jesus Christ, in the love of the Father, and the communion of the Holy Spirit!

> *"Too many of us simply don't know what we're missing because we do not know what we had."*—Robert Tuttle on original perfection[6]

> *"Too many of us simply don't know what we must be becoming NOW because we do not know what we will soon be!"* —Craig Green on restored perfection

Lesson Seven—*The Heart of Control* (Matt. 15:10-20)

1. "HEART" = Character, Nature, Being, "Ontology"

2. The difference between a *Symptom* and the *Source*, a *Band-Aid* and a *Cure*

3. The difference between an outward act (religion) and an inward transformation

4. What proceeds out of a new heart should be radically different from what proceeded out of the old.

5. *We must be changed to the core!*

6. *The Game of Control:* All humans "naturally" play it.

7. *The Source of Control:* Satan

8. *The Breadth of Control:* From Genesis to Revelation

9. *The Opposite of Control:* God's very nature and character!

10. *Overcoming Control:* By growing up into mature Christianity

11. *The End of Control:* Perfection restored (Even here and now!)

As the *Heart of Control* is removed, **and the *Heart of Jesus* implanted!**

a. Mutual Submission (must be expressed in service to others)

b. Servant Ministry (only possible in a place of mutual submission)

c. DAILY relationship with the Lord—Dancing with God! (Worship!)

d. Daily dying to self and true repentance (rejection of old heart)

e. Going on to perfection (loving God with all of our heart, soul, and strength)

—Attributed to John Wesley
(By perfection, Wesley meant loving God and neighbor
perfectly in this life—with all of our heart, soul,
and strength).

Learning Outcomes Review:

Lesson One—*The Game of Control* (Eph. 4:11-16)

1. Since the Fall, *all* humans have played an unwinnable game, the game of control, trying to be "god" over each other by dominating, intimidating or manipulating to get their way.

2. The True God, Father, Son and Holy Spirit, *never* plays this game; it's not *in* Him!

3. The game of control is like Rock/Paper/Scissors
Rock = Domination
Paper = Manipulation
Scissors = Intimidation

4. Believers need deep (core) inner healing, including God's help to stop "playing the game" of control.

5. Servant ministry is one of God's primary ways to help us stop playing the game of control, and in order to be servant ministers, we must be equipped within the Church.

Lesson Two—*The Source of Control* (Gen. 1:26-28)

1. *Dominion* and *control* are diametrically opposed, because the characters of *God* and *satan* are diametrically opposed. In the beginning, humans had *dominion*—because we reflected perfectly the image of God

2. God is 3 in 1—manifesting perfect, selfless, loving, giving, humble **relationship** *within* Himself as Trinity. The early Church fathers called this *Perichoresis*—The Divine Choreography or Dance

3. Humans were originally designed to have Perichoresis with God, each other, and within themselves. Perfect harmony. Perfect relationship. Perfect unity. Perfect love.

4. Satan fell, and then, when Adam and Eve followed suit, human nature took on the character of satan (manifest in control), and lost the character and nature of God (manifest in dominion).

5. Disciples (apprentices) of Jesus are being restored to our original righteousness, character, nature, and dominion, by His Sacrifice, grace, love, and Spirit—this is very good news!

Lesson Three—*The Breadth of Control* (Luke 4:1-13)

1. The unholy trinity of satan's character (control) is seen throughout Scripture; but Jesus, the second Adam, resisted satan's temptations, and in Him we are being restored to God's character!

2. *"Do not love the world....For all that is in the world—the lust of the flesh* [domination], *the lust of the eyes* [manipulation], *and the pride of life* [intimidation]—*is not of the Father..."* (1 John 2:15-16).

3. Jesus warns the Church that control in the Church—Nicolaitan-ism (domination), Balaam-ism (manipulation), and Jezebel-ism (intimidation)—must be exposed, repented of, and never tolerated.

4. "Satan's last stand" will involve the demonic personification of evil in an unholy trinity of *domination* through "the beast," *intimidation* through the "false prophet," and *manipulation* through "the dragon." The end times will be marked by a crescendo of control in all its ugliness.

Lesson Four—*The Opposite of Control* (Eph. 5:21)

1. The opposite of *Domination* is **Love**, which describes the **Father** (and *all* of the Trinity!)

2. The opposite of *Intimidation* is **Humility**, which describes the **Son** (and *all* of the Trinity!)

3. The opposite of *Manipulation* is **Truth**, which describes the **Holy Spirit** (and *all* of the Trinity!)

4. The KEY to living a life OPPOSITE of Domination/Intimi-dation/Manipulation (Control) is to live a life *"submitted one to another,"* a life of Love, Humility, and Truth *in relationship.*

5. The Bible gives us many examples of transformed lives, former control freaks that became free from being controlled and controlling, such as Peter, Paul, and James.

6. True and normal Christianity must include transformation away from satan's character, and toward God's character. Disciples: Confess, repent, and receive.

Lesson Five—*Overcoming Control* (Rev. 12:7-12)

1. **Overcoming by the blood**—satan can't *manipulate* believers who know they are *accepted* by the blood. And people lay down the "right" to manipulate as they rest in the power of the blood. (Victory in the emotional realm)

2. **Overcoming by their testimony**—satan can't *intimidate* believers who know they are *right* by the Word...And people lay down their "right" to intimidate as testifying to the Word takes precedence in their lives. (Victory in the spiritual realm)

3. **Overcoming by loving Jesus more than life itself**—satan can't *dominate* believers who know they've already *won* in Jesus and don't fear death. And people lay down the "right" to dominate as their love for Jesus exceeds their fear of death. (Victory in the physical realm)

4. **The only way to become an "Overcoming" Christian is to**:
   a. Crucify the flesh.
   b. Ask for and receive Spirit baptism.
   c. Grow from being a "milk" Christian to being a "meat" Christian.
   d. Grow in the blood-assuring, Word-testifying, and life-sacrificing, loving character of Jesus Christ!

Lesson Six—*The End of Control* (Rev. 22:1-5)

1. Perfection is coming again – and is the only reasonable goal for a believer *now*.

2. Perfect:
   Life
   Provision
   Unity
   Relationship
   Revelation
   Dominion

3. We have no excuse to settle for anything less than perfection in our lives *now!* Jesus is perfection! He is here! The Tree of Life and the fruit of the Spirit are ours to "taste and see" *now!* The "fig leaves" of satan's character have been replaced by the tunic of Christ's perfect sacrifice and character!

4. NOT: "I'm going on to Heaven in the *sweet by-and-by*"
   BUT RATHER: I'm going to *be* Heaven in the *sweet here-and-now!*

Lesson Seven—*The Heart of Control* (Matt. 15:10-20)
CHANGE MY HEART, O GOD! MAY I BE LIKE YOU!

Post-teaching Review and Critique

Please share what you considered the main focus of each lesson, any comments or criticisms, and any suggestions for improvement.

Lesson 1—The Game of Control.

_____

_____

_____

Lesson 2—The Source of Control.

_____

_____

_____

Lesson 3—The Breadth of Control.

_____

_____

_____

Lesson 4—The Opposite of Control.

_____

_____

_____

Lesson 5—Overcoming Control.

_____

_____

_____

Lesson 6—The End of Control.

_____

_____

_____

Lesson 7—The Heart of Control.

_____

_____

_____

A key goal of this project was to promote "mutual submission as expressed through servant ministry." Please define:

Mutual Submission

_____

_____

Servant Ministry

_____

_____

The connection between the two

_____

_____

Please describe any experiences of God's grace, transformation, revelation, or other experiences and encounters with Him related to being part of this teaching:

_____

_____

_____

_____

Were you able to discern what control type you *primarily* operate(d) in?   YES   NO

If so, which one?
Domination   Intimidation   Manipulation

Any comments?

_____

_____

_____

_____

_____

Do you sense any change in your: inner being/character/nature/
heart—by being a part of this course?   YES   NO

If so, please describe.

_____

_____

_____

_____

_____

Would you recommend this course to others?   YES   NO

Why or why not?

_____

_____

_____

_____

_____

*I sincerely thank you for any and all comments, and pray the very
character of God will be ever more formed in you and me, to the glory
of His glorious name!*

—Craig A. Green

ENDNOTES

Chapter One

1. Ontology is a theological term meaning the study one's nature and character—a person's very being.
2. This argument will form the core of the second chapter of this project, as the author looks at the ontological and Trinitarian being of the Godhead, and the absence of anything resembling "control."
3. This is insinuated in the text both by satan's appearing as a serpent, and by the statement that *"the serpent was more cunning than any beast of the field which the Lord God had made"* (Gen. 3:1).
4. The manipulation is implicit in satan's motives in asking in Genesis 3:1, *"Has God indeed said, 'You shall not eat of every tree of the garden'?"* The cunning creation of doubt in another's mind is one form of manipulation.
5. Domination is clearly seen in Genesis 3:4-5 as satan boldly lies to Eve, stating, *"You will not surely die."*
6. That dominion is connected to God's image is made clear in Genesis 1:26. That control is a reflection of satan's image is intimated in Genesis 3, as well as in satan's temptation of Jesus in the wilderness (see Matt. 4; Luke 4).

7. Eric Reed, "Leadership Surveys Church Conflict," *Leadership*, Fall 2004, 25.

8. George Bloomer, *Spiritual Warfare* (New Kensington, PA: Whitaker House, 2004), 47-99.

9. Mark Rutland, *Power* (Lake Mary, FL: Charisma House, 2004), 38.

10. Ibid., 41.

11. Rock/Paper/Scissors, also known as Roshambo, is played all over the world, has been used (in England) as a legal method to settle disputes and enter into contracts, and is played in international tournaments sanctioned by the World RPS Society. Websites abound, as do strategy books and training courses.

12. Carol Suplicki and Gina Molino, eds., *Webster's Dictionary and Thesaurus* (Nichols Publishing Group, 1999), 236.

13. Ibid., 515.

14. Ibid., 449.

15. Rod Smith, "Three Poisons for Love: Manipulation, Intimidation, and Domination," March 15, 2006, Difficult Relationships, http://rodesmith.wordpress.com/.

16. Ibid.

17. Robert G. Tuttle. Interviewed by author December 2, 2006. In-person interview. First United Methodist Church, Livingston, TN.

18. Ibid.

19. Leon Van Rooyen, "The Church of Dry Bones," *Charisma* and *Christian Life*, June 2006, 63-66.

20. Les Parrott III, *The Control Freak* (Wheaton, IL: Tyndale House, 2000), 21.

21. David Gergen, "Bad News for Bullies," *U.S. News and World Report*, June 19, 2006, 54.

22. Jim Collins, *Good to Great* (New York: HarperCollins Publishers, Inc., 2001), 12-13.

23. Rodney J. Hunter, ed., *Dictionary of Pastoral Care and Counseling* (Nashville, TN: Abingdon Press, 1990), 661.

Chapter Two

1. Robert G. Tuttle, *Sanctity Without Starch* (Lexington: Bristol Books, 1992), 23.
2. *The Journal of the Rev. John Wesley,* 142.
3. Donald K. McKim, *Westminster Dictionary of Theological Terms* (Louisville: Westminster John Knox Press, 1996), 195.
4. *The New England Primer 1777* (Aledo, TX: WallBuilder Press, 1991).
5. Dallas Willard, *The Great Omission* (New York: HarperCollins Publishers, Inc., 2006), xiii.
6. Scriptures that help illuminate the Trinity, and unity within the Trinity, include Matthew 3:16-17, 28:19; John 10:30, 14:26;, 15:26; Romans 1:4, 5:5-6, 8:2-3, 9, 16-17, 14:17-18, 15:16-17, 30; 1 Corinthians 12:4-6; 2 Corinthians 13:14; and 1 Peter 1:2.
7. Gilbert Bilezikian, *Christianity 101* (Grand Rapids, MI: Zondervan Publishing House, 1993), 30.
8. Ibid.
9. Ibid.
10. Ibid.
11. Timothy Ware, *The Orthodox Church* (London: Penguin Books, 1993), 218-219.
12. Thomas C. Oden, *The Word of Life: Systematic Theology Vol. II.* (New York: HarperCollins Publishers, Inc., 1989), 66.
13. Ibid., 71.
14. John Ortberg, *Everybody's Normal Till You Get To Know Them* (Grand Rapids, MI: Zondervan, 2003), 35.
15. I believe this is the heart of the age-long battle of satan against God: always the manipulating, dominating, intimidating lies about who God is and what God is like, as first revealed in Genesis 3.
16. Oden, *The Word of Life: Systematic Theology Vol. II,* 186.
17. F.L. Cross and E.A. Livingstone, eds., *The Oxford Dictionary of the Christian Church* (New York: Oxford University Press, 1990), 237.

18. Ibid.

19. Ware, *The Orthodox Church*, 23.

20. Ibid., 22.

21. This becomes obvious with even a cursory review of Catholic, Orthodox, or Protestant theological texts, ancient or modern.

22. Dale T. Irvin and Scott W. Sunquist, *History of the World Christian Movement, Volume I: Earliest Christianity to 1453* (Maryknoll, NY: Orbis Books, 2001), 184-185.

23. Gregory Nazianzen, *Orat. XXXI.3, A Select Library of the Nicene and Post-Nicene Fathers of the Christian Church* (New York: Christian, 1887-1900). 2nd Series VII, 318.

24. Carlton R. Young, ed., *The United Methodist Hymnal* (Nashville, TN: The United Methodist Publishing House, 1989), 880.

25. Gregory Nazianzen, *Introduction to Theological Orations,* reproduced in Christian Classics Ethereal Library, Nicene and Post-Nicene Fathers, Series II, Volume VII.

26. Schaff-Wace, ed., *Post-Nicene Fathers of the Christian Church* (London, trans. By Blomfield Jackson, 1894) Series II, Volume VIII.

27. Gregory of Nyssa, *To Eustathius,* Reproduced in Christian Classics Ethereal Library, Nicene and Post-Nicene Fathers, Series II, Volume V.

28. A term used by the author to convey the reality and reliability of the Living Word, as He animates Scripture to us through vibrant relationship. While the Scripture is, of course, without error, it remains only words on paper unless and until it becomes the Word, alive and vibrant in and by relationship.

29. Thomas C. Oden, *The Living God: Systematic Theology Vol. I*, 210.

30. Ibid., 210-211.

31. Ibid., 211.

32. Ibid.

33. The author of this project studied the antonyms of the three manifestations of control: Domination, Manipulation, and Intimidation, and found Love (see 1 John 4:8), Truth (see John 16:13), and Humility (see Phil. 2:5-11) to be not only antonyms of control, but biblical descriptions of the nature (ontology) of the Godhead.

34. C. Baxter Kruger, *The Great Dance* (Vancouver: Regent College Publishing, 2005), 22-23.

35. See Genesis 3:11-13. Implicit in the text, as well as in this researcher's project, is the truth that blame can be used as a form of manipulation, producing guilt; as a form of domination, producing capitulation; and as a form of intimidation, producing fear.

36. Jack W. Hayford, ed., *The Hayford Bible Handbook* (Nashville, TN: Thomas Nelson, Inc., 1995), 680.

Chapter Three

1. Ezek. 28:14, footnote in the *New Spirit Filled Life Bible*.

2. Bilezikian, *Christianity 101*, 39.

3. Isa. 14:12-21, footnote in the *New Spirit Filled Life Bible*.

4. Donald K. McKim, *Westminster Dictionary of Theological* Terms (Louisville: Westminster John Knox Press, 1996), 165.

5. Ibid., 248.

6. 2 Cor. 11:14.

7. Marilyn Hickey, "Kingdom Dynamics: Isaiah 14:12-14, Lucifer," in the *New Spirit Filled Life Bible*, ed. Jack W. Hayford and others (Nashville: Thomas Nelson Bibles, 2002), 891.

8. Ezek. 28:13, footnote in the *New Spirit Filled Life Bible*.

9. Walter A. Elwell, ed., *Evangelical Commentary on the Bible* (Grand Rapids, MI: Baker Book House 1989), 579.

10. Ibid., 1228.

11. While Scripture makes reference to the antichrist and to antichrist's in several places (see 1 John 2:18; 1 John 2:22; 1 John 4:3; 2 John 7), to be opposed to Christ is to be anti-trinity, and all that constitutes His character, being, and relational ontology. Domination, manipulation, and intimidation are just such an antichrist and false trinity—an anti-trinity.

12. Elwell, *Evangelical Commentary on the Bible*, 1216-1217.

13. Bruce, *The International Bible Commentary*, 1616.

14. Elwell, *Evangelical Commentary on the Bible*, 13.

15. Barry J. Beitzel, Chief Consultant, *Biblica The Bible Atlas* (Lane Cove, Australia: Global Book Publishing, 2006), 95.

16. Bruce, 117.
17. Watchman Nee, *The Spiritual Man* (New York: Christian Fellowship Publishers, Inc., 1977), 46.
18. Ibid.
19. Ibid.
20. Dennis and Rita Bennett, *Trinity of Man* (Green Forest, AR: New Leaf Press, 1987), 39-48.
21. Gen. 3:6, footnote in *The New Oxford Annotated Bible.*
22. Gen. 3:7, footnote in the *New Spirit Filled Life Bible.*
23. Aryeh Kaplan, trans. *The Torah Anthology* (New York: Moznaim Publishing Corp., 1988), 262.
24. Peter Michas, Robert Vander Maten, and Christie Michas, *The Rod of an Almond Tree in God's Master Plan* (Mukilteo, WA: WinePress Publishing, 1997), 100.
25. Charles Simpson, "Kingdom Dynamics: Genesis 3:21, The Blood, the Covering," in the *New Spirit Filled Life Bible*, ed. Jack W. Hayford and others (Nashville: Thomas Nelson Bibles, 2002), 10.
26. Ibid.
27. This insight is not original in terms of the obvious connections between the tripartite temptations of the first and second Adams; what is unique to this project is the correlation between the temptations and domination, intimidation, and manipulation.
28. Nouwen, *In the Name of Jesus*, 38-39.
29. Ibid., 55-60.
30. Luke 4, footnote in *The Nelson Study Bible* and *New Spirit Filled Life Bible.*
31. Luke 10:19, footnote in the *New Spirit Filled Life Bible.*
32. Bruce, *The International Bible Commentary*, 1204.
33. Luke 10:18, footnote in the *New Spirit Filled Bible.*
34. Luke 10:18, 19, footnote in *The Life Application Bible.*
35. Luke 10:19-20, footnote in *The Nelson Study Bible.*
36. Jack W. Hayford, "Kingdom Dynamics: Revelation 12:10, 11, Agelong Warfare," in the *New Spirit Filled Life Bible*, 1833.
37. Ibid.
38. This argument, offered by this researcher, flows from comparing this passage with the tripartite temptations of Adam and Jesus,

the human trinity of body/soul/spirit, and the false trinity of domination, intimidation, and manipulation. While many have written concerning the implications of this passage, this precise interpretation is a product of this research project.

39. Ibid.
40. Ibid.
41. Marva Dawn, *Powers, Weakness, and the Tabernacling of* God (Grand Rapids, MI: William B. Eerdmans Publishing Co., 2001), 41.
42. John 14:30, footnote in the *New Spirit Filled Bible.*

Chapter Four

1. Jack W. Hayford, Ed., *The Hayford Bible Handbook* (Nashville, TN: Thomas Nelson, Inc., 1995), 788.
2. Dennis and Rita Bennett, *Trinity of Man* (Green Forest, AR: New Leaf Press, 1987), 54-55.
3. Donald K. McKim, *Westminster Dictionary of Theological Terms* (Louisville: Westminster John Knox Press, 1996), 195.
4. Bennett, *Trinity of Man*, 63-68.
5. Dietrich Bonhoeffer, *The Cost of Discipleship* (New York: Collier Books, 1963), 47.

Chapter Six

1. Carol Suplicki and Gina Molino, eds., *Webster's Dictionary and Thesaurus* (Nichols Publishing Group, 1999), 236.
2. Ibid., 449.
3. Ibid., 515.

Chapter Eleven

1. Note: Jim Hill, "What a Day That Will Be," Ben Speer Music, 1955, 1983.
2. Robert G. Tuttle, *Sanctity Without Starch* (Lexington: Bristol Books, 1992), 23.

Chapter Thirteen

1. Charles E. Blair, "Introduction to 'Job,'" in the *New Spirit Filled Life Bible,* ed. Jack W. Hayford and others (Nashville, TN: Thomas Nelson Bibles, 2002), 646.
2. Blair, 645.
3. "Word Wealth," Job 1:6 "Satan," in the *New Spirit Filled Life Bible,* 648.
4. Job 1:6-2:7, footnote in the *New Spirit Filled Life Bible.*
5. Elwell, *Evangelical Commentary on the Bible,* 344.
6. Job 4:13, footnote in the *New Spirit Filled Life Bible.*
7. Elwell, *Evangelical Commentary on the Bible,* 344.
8. Ibid., 345.
9. Blair, "Introduction to 'Job,'" in the *New Spirit Filled Life Bible,* 645.
10. Frank E. Gaebelein, ed. *The Expositor's Bible Commentary Vol. 4,* 905.
11. Elwell, *Evangelical Commentary on the Bible,* 347.
12. Job 11:1-20 footnote in *The Nelson Study Bible.*
13. Job 32:1-22, footnote in the *New Spirit Filled Life Bible.*
14. Blair, "Introduction to 'Job'" in the *New Spirit Filled Life Bible,* 646-647.

Appendix

1. Carol Suplicki and Gina Molino, eds., *Webster's Dictionary and Thesaurus* (Nichols Publishing Group, 1999), 236.
2. Ibid., 449.
3. C. Baxter Kruger, *The Great Dance* (Vancouver: Regent College Publishing, 2005), 22-23.
4. Gregory Nazianzen, *Introduction to Theological Orations,* reproduced in Christian Classics Ethereal Library, Nicene and Post-Nicene Fathers, Series II, Volume VII.
5. Robert G. Tuttle, *Sanctity Without Starch* (Lexington: Bristol Books, 1992), 23.
6. Ibid.

BIBLIOGRAPHY

Books

Arterburn, Stephen and Jack Felton. *Toxic Faith*. Colorado Springs. WaterBrook Press, 2001.

Athanasius of Alexandria. *Select Treatises of S. Athanasius*. Oxford: James Parker and Co., 1877.

Beck, James R. and Craig L. Blomberg, eds. *Two Views on Women in Ministry*. Grand Rapids: Zondervan Publishing House, 2001.

Beitzel, Barry J. Chief Consultant. *Biblica: The Bible Atlas*. Lane Cove, Australia: Global Book Publishing, 2006.

Bennett, Dennis and Rita. *Trinity of Man*. Green Forest, AR: New Leaf Press, 1987.

Bevere, John. *Thus Saith the Lord?* Lake Mary, FL: Creation House, 1999.

Bilezikian, Gilbert. *Christianity 101*. Grand Rapids: Zondervan Publishing House, 1993.

Blair, Charles E. "Introduction to 'Job,'" in the *New Spirit Filled Life Bible*. Ed. Jack W. Hayford and others. Nashville: Thomas Nelson Bibles, 2002.

Bloomer, George. *Authority Abusers*. New Kensington, PA: Whitaker House, 1995.

———. *Spiritual Warfare*. New Kensington, PA: Whitaker House, 2004.

Blue, Ken. *Healing Spiritual Abuse*. Downers Grove, IL: InterVarsity Press, 1993.

Bonhoeffer, Dietrich. *The Cost of Discipleship*. New York: Macmillan Publishing Company, 1963.

Bruce, F. F. ed. *The International Bible Commentary*. Grand Rapids: Zondervan Publishing House, 1986.

Burchett, Dave. *When Bad Christians Happen to Good People*. Colorado Springs: WaterBrook Press, 2002.

Calvin, John. *Institutes of the Christian Religion*. Ed. John McNeill, no. 1. Philadelphia: Westminster, 1960.

Chadwick, H. trans. *Origen: Contra Celsum,* Oxford: Oxford Press, 1965, 4.

Clarke, Adam. *A Commentary and Critical Notes,* Vol. 4. Nashville: Abingdon Press.

Cloud, Henry and John Townsend. *Boundaries*. Grand Rapids: Zondervan, 1992.

Collins, Jim. *Good to Great*. New York: HarperCollins Publishers, Inc., 2001.

Cordeiro, Wayne. *Doing Church as a Team*. Ventura, CA: Regal Books, 2001.

Cross, F. L. and E .A. Livingstone, eds. *The Oxford Dictionary of the Christian Church.* New York: Oxford University Press, 1990.

Daugherty, Billy Joe. "Kingdom Dynamics: Ephesians 4:11, 12, Equipping Believers," in the *New Spirit Filled Life Bible.* Ed. Jack W. Hayford and others. Nashville: Thomas Nelson Bibles, 2002.

Dawn, Marva J. *Powers, Weakness, and the Tabernacling of God.* Grand Rapids: William B. Eerdmans, 2001.

Dupont, Marc. *Toxic Churches.* Grand Rapids.: Chosen Books, 2004.

Eicher, James P., John E. Jones, and William L Bearley. *Post-Heroic Leadership.* Amherst, MA: HRD Press, 1999.

Eldridge, Robert. *A History of The First Methodist Church.* Livingston, TN: Enterprise Printing Company, 1962.

Elwell, Walter A. ed. *Evangelical Commentary on the Bible.* Grand Rapids: Baker Book House 1989.

Evans, Patricia. *Controlling People.* Avon, MA: Adams Media, 2002.

Fischer, John. *12 Steps for the Recovering Pharisee.* Bloomington, MN: Bethany House Publishers, 2000.

Gaebelein, Frank E., ed. *The Expositor's Bible Commentary,* Vol. 4. Grand Rapids: Zondervan Publishing House, 1986.

Godwin, Rick. *Exposing Witchcraft in the Church.* Lake Mary, FL: Charisma House, 1997.

Greenleaf, Robert K. *The Power of Servant-Leadership.* San Francisco: Berrett-Koehler Publishers, 1998.

Griffith, R. Marie. *God's Daughters: Evangelical Women and the Power of Submission.* Berkley, CA: University of California Press, 1997.

Grudem, Wayne. *Systematic Theology.* Grand Rapids: Zondervan Publishing House, 1994.

Gustafson, Gerrit. *The Adventure of Worship.* Grand Rapids: Chosen Books, 2006.

Hayford, Jack W., "Kingdom Dynamics: Revelation 12:10, 11, Agelong Warfare," in the *New Spirit Filled Life Bible,* 1833.

———. *Living the Spirit Formed Life.* Ventura, CA: Regal Books, 2001.

———. *The Hayford Bible Handbook.* Nashville: Thomas Nelson, Inc., 1995.

Hickey, Marilyn. "Kingdom Dynamics: Isaiah 14:12-14, Lucifer," in the *New Spirit Filled Life Bible.* Ed. Jack W. Hayford, et al. Nashville: Thomas Nelson Bibles, 2002.

Irvin, Dale T. and Scott W. Sunquist. *History of the World Christian Movement, Volume I: Earliest Christianity to 1453.* Maryknoll, NY: Orbis Books, 2001.

Johnson, David and Jeff VanVonderen. *The Subtle Power of Spiritual Abuse.* Minneapolis: Bethany House Publishers, 1991.

Johnson, Jan. *Community and Submission.* Downers Grove, IL: InterVarsity Press, 2003.

Kaplan, Aryeh, trans. *The Torah Anthology.* New York: Moznaim Publishing Corp., 1988.

Kruger, C. Baxter. *Across All Worlds.* Jackson, MS: Perichoresis Press, 2004.

———. *God Is For Us.* Jackson, MS: Perichoresis Press, 2000.

———. *The Great Dance.* Vancouver: Regent College Publishing, 2005.

Lawford, G. Ross. *The Quest for Authentic Power.* San Francisco: Berrett-Koehler Publishers, Inc., 2002.

Littauer, Marita. *Your Spiritual Personality.* San Francisco: Josey-Bass, 2005.

Malone, Paul B. *Abuse 'Em and Lose 'Em.* Annandale, VI: Synergy Press, 1990.

McKim, Donald K. *Westminster Dictionary of Theological Terms.* Louisville: Westminster John Knox Press, 1996.

Michas, Peter, Robert Vander Maten, and Christie Michas. *The Rod of an Almond Tree in God's Master Plan.* Mukilteo, WA: WinePress Publishing, 1997.

Moore, Keith. *Servant Leadership in the Twenty-First Century.* Garden City, NY: Morgan James Publishing, 2005.

Nee, Watchman. *The Spiritual Man.* New York: Christian Fellowship Publishers, Inc., 1977.

Nouwen, Henri J.M. *In the Name of Jesus.* New York: Crossroad Publishing Company, 1994.

Oden, Thomas C. *The Living God: Systematic Theology Vol. I.* New York: HarperCollins Publishers, Inc., 1987.

———. *The Word of Life: Systematic Theology Vol. II.* New York: HarperCollins Publishers, Inc., 1989.

Origen. Chadwick, trans. *Origen: Contra Celsum.* Oxford: Oxford Press, 1965.

Ortberg, John. *Everybody's Normal Till You Get to Know Them.* Grand Rapids: Zondervan, 2003.

Parrott III, Les. *The Control Freak.* Wheaton, IL: Tyndale House, 2000.

Peterson, Beth E. *People Who Play God*. Philadelphia: Xlibris Corporation, 2003.

Pinkham, Wesley M. "Relational Theology," Chapter 10: *Sin, Good & Evil, Heaven & Hell, Devil and Angels*. Unpublished Book: Journey to the Heart, 2004.

Russell, Jeffery Burton. *Satan: The Early Christian Tradition*. Ithaca, NY: Cornell University Press, 1981.

Rutland, Mark. *Power*. Lake Mary, FL: Charisma House, 2004.

Scazzero, Peter. *The Emotionally Healthy Church*. Grand Rapids: Zondervan, 2003.

Simpson, Charles. "Kingdom Dynamics: Genesis 3:21, The Blood, the Covering," in the *New Spirit Filled Life Bible*. Ed. Jack W. Hayford, et al. Nashville: Thomas Nelson Bibles, 2002.

Stern, David H. *Jewish New Testament Commentary*. Clarksville, Maryland: Jewish New Testament Publications, 1992.

Suplicki, Carol, and Gina Molino, eds. *Webster's Dictionary and Thesaurus*. Nichols Publishing Group, 1999.

Synan, Vinson. *The Century of the Holy Spirit*. Nashville: Thomas Nelson, Inc., 2001.

Teykl, Terry. *The Presence Based Church*. Muncie, IN: Prayer Point Press, 2003.

Tuttle, Robert G. *Sanctity Without Starch*. Lexington: Bristol Books, 1992.

Ware, Timothy. *The Orthodox Church*. London: Penguin Books, 1993.

Wesley, John. *A Plain Account of Christian Perfection*. London: Epworth Press, 1993.

————. *The Journal of the Rev. John Wesley, A.M.* Ed. Nehemiah Curnock London: Epworth, 1909-16; rpt 1938.

————. *Works,* Vol. 9.

Willard, Dallas. *The Great Omission.* New York: HarperCollins Publishers, 2006.

Wills, Dick. *Waking to God's Dream.* Nashville: Abingdon Press, 1999.

Young, Carlton R., ed. *The United Methodist Hymnal.* Nashville: The United Methodist Publishing House, 1989.

Periodicals

Cope, Brad, ed. *Spirit,* April, 2007, 30.

Gergen, David. "Bad News for Bullies." *U.S. News and World Report,* June 19, 2006, 54.

Lattin, Don. "How Spiritual Journey Ended in Destruction." *San Francisco Chronicle,* November 18, 2003, 1A, pg. 1.

Reed, Eric. "Leadership Surveys Church Conflict." *Leadership,* Fall 2004, 25.

Spanks, Lee. "The Danger of Applause." *Circuit Rider,* March-April, 2007, 12.

Tiansay, Eric and Adrienne S. Gaines. "Derek Prince, Charismatic Author, Bible Teacher, Dies in Jerusalem," *Charisma and Christian Life.* November 2003.

Van Rooyen, Leon. "The Church of Dry Bones." *Charisma and Christian Life,* June 2006, 63-66.

Wunderink, Susan. "What to Do With a Former Informant." *Christianity Today,* March, 2007, 68-70.

E-Form Books

Edwards, Jonathan. An Unpublished Essay on the Trinity. Reproduced in the *Christians Classics Ethereal Library.*

Gregory Nazianzen, Introduction to Theological Orations, reproduced in *Christian Classics Ethereal Library, Nicene and Post-Nicene Fathers,* Series II, Volume VII.

———. Orat.XXXI.3, *A Select Library of the Nicene and Post-Nicene Fathers of the Christian Church.* New York: Christian, 1887-1900. 2nd Series VII.

Gregory of Nyssa. To Eustathius. Reproduced in *Christian Classics Ethereal Library, Nicene and Post-Nicene Fathers,* Series II, Volume V.

Schaff-Wace, ed. *Post-Nicene Fathers of the Christian Church.* London, trans. By Blomfield Jackson, 1894. Series II, Volume VIII.

Other

Smith, Rod. "Three Poisons for Love: Manipulation, Intimidation, and Domination," March 15, 2006, Difficult Relationships, http://rodesmith.wordpress.com/

Tuttle, Robert G. Interviewed by author, December 2, 2006. In-person interview. First United Methodist Church, Livingston, Tennessee.